D0933261

VITALIS

BIBLIOTHECA
BOHEMICA

Malá Strana Stories

Stephenovi

Romana

1.6. 2000

Jan Neruda

Malá Strana Stories

A Week in a Quiet House

Vitalis

© Vitalis, Prague 1999
    U Lužického semináře 19
    CZ-118 00 Praha 1
    e-mail: Vitalis@telecom. cz

Original Czech Title: Povídky Malostranské
Translation: Petr Kopet
Editing: Karen Reppin, Marc Reppin
Translation from German of the two poems
in story 3, and jacket text: Karen Reppin
Illustrations including: Karel Hruška
Typography: CADIS
Printing and Binding: FINIDR, Český Těšín
ISBN 80-85938-19-7

A Week in a Quiet House

1867

Contents

1 In a Nightgown

We sense that we are in a completely sealed off room. Pitch darkness surrounds us, not even the tiniest cracks allow the dimmest light to penetrate; all around is such darkness that if we believed just for a moment that we were seeing anything light in front of our eyes, it would be the red halo of our own thoughts.

The senses are heightened, perceiving even the slightest signs of life. Our sense of smell tells us that the room is filled with a greasy odour of sorts, a blend of everyday smells. One moment we think we smell mostly pine or fir, the next moment tallow and lard, and then again dried prunes, cumin, even brandy, garlic, and so forth. Our sense of hearing is touched by the ticking of the clock. It must be an old wall clock with a thin and, in all likelihood, bent tin disc at the end of its long pendulum; at times, the pendulum stutters in the telling of its tale and the disc shivers slightly. Even this stutter is repeated at regular intervals and becomes monotonous.

Meanwhile, we hear the breathing of sleepers. There must be several of them. The sounds of breathing intertwine, never quite coming together; it is as if one was fading away while the other intensified, one was stuttering along with the pendulum while the other rushed on, and into all of this a stronger, heavier sigh from elsewhere suddenly sighs again, like a new chapter of sleep.

Now the clock too suddenly gives a sigh and a whir. After that whirring quotation mark, the pendulum seems to move more quietly. One of the sleepers stirs and the blanket rustles; the sleeper's wooden bed creaks.

The clock gives another whir, 'one-two' resonates quickly one right after the other in a sonorous metallic sound, followed by another 'one-two' and cookoos in a deep voice. The sleeping person stirs again. The sleeper can be heard sitting up and pulling off the covers. Her leg brushes against the side of the bed – now she fumbles about with a heavy slipper, we realize that she already has both slippers on. She starts to move and takes a few tentative steps. She comes to a halt again; something crackles under her hand groping along a wooden board, it must be matches. Several times she strikes a match, several times phosphorous smoke flashes up; another strike, the little wooden stick breaks, the person grumbles. Some new strikes, and finally a small flame whirls and the light from it spreads over a figure clad in a nightgown. The small flame flickers again, but the bony old hand has already brought it to a glass filled with water and oil, in which a cork with a black wick floats on the surface. The wick lights up like a little star. The match falls to the ground and the little star swiftly grows. Above it stands a figure clad in a nightgown, an old woman, yawning and rubbing her sleepy eyes.

The figure is standing beside a table pushed right up to a darkly painted wooden partition, which divides the whole room in two. The range of the lamplight does not reach beyond the partition, only one part of the room can be seen – our sense of smell, however, was not mistaken, we are in a grocer's storeroom. This same room is clearly being used as living quarters as well as a shop. The store is supplied with a great variety of provisions, as befits such a place, an abundance of sacks with common goods, filled bushels and wicker baskets tower above the sacks, plaits and bunches hang from the walls.

The woman shivered in the cool of the night, took the lamp from the table and put it on a counter full of jars of fresh and clarified butter, scales and bunches of garlic and onions dangling from above. She sat down at the counter, curled her legs up to her chin and reached for a box filled with thread, scissors and other odds and ends. She took out the thread and everything else, and finally got to the papers and books at the bottom. She paid no attention to the papers covered mostly with numbers but took out one of the books and opened it. It was a dream-book, the so-called "large" dream-book. She became fully absorbed in turning the pages, now reading, now yawning a bit, and then reading again.

By now, there could be heard only the measured breath of a sleeper behind the partition; the second sleeper, awoken by either the noise or the shimmer of light, stirred in his bed.

"What's that?" a cranky, old male voice grumbled from the other side.

The woman did not answer.

"Are you alright, woman?"

"Go back to sleep," replied the woman, "I'm fine, only cold!" She yawned.

"So what are you tinkering with over there?"

"I had a dream about my late father, I would forget it come morning. It was a beautiful dream, I've never dreamed anything like it before. It's so cold, and it's June!" She continued reading and shook her head. There was silence for a short while.

Then, "What time is it?" came from behind the wall again.

"Past two."

The breathing of the third sleeper was becoming irregular, the loud talking was waking him up.

"Get on with it then, so we can get some sleep! All you can think of is your lottery!"

"Right, you're never left alone in peace around here. Get some sleep and leave me alone."

The breathing behind the wall ended with a heavy sigh. The sleeper in the third bed was awake now, too. The old man continued to grumble, "My reveling son doesn't get home before midnight, and after midnight I get woken up by this racket, what a life!"

"You just don't quit, do you? I slave away and for what? My own husband just grumbles away ... if you could at least control your son that would be something. I'm fed up with all this!"

"You control him, he's yours too. Control the reveler!"

"What do you want, Father?" asked a young male voice.

"Quiet, shut up, who are you to ask questions!"

"But I really don't understand ..."

"Oh, he doesn't understand," ridiculed the old man, "the scoundrel!"

"But – "

"Quiet!!"

"So he's talking back to you, is he, what a wonderful son we have, we sure raised ourselves a treat!" stated the woman and yawned again.

"Son? That's no son, that's a robber of our health!"

"How do I rob you when I'm asleep?"

"You rogue!"

"What a scamp!"

"He's a scoundrel!"

14

"A scoundrel!"

The son started quietly whistling "Oh Matylda."

"Look at him, he's even laughing at us, on top of everything!"

"God's punishment will be swift to come upon him," said the woman, taking some chalk and writing the numbers 16, 23, and 8 on the wooden partition. "We will still live to see it, but I wish I was no longer among the living then." She packed up the box, blew out the light and groped her way back to bed. "He'll suffer for it, but it will be too late then. Now, will you be quiet?"

The son fell silent.

"You will try to dig us out of our graves with a pin, but all in vain; with a pin, I tell you, a pin!"

"Come on, woman, leave the pins alone and go to sleep, I'm so sleepy!"

"Well, I'm the one to get the blame, of course. Oh God, how do I deserve this!"

"You drive me crazy!"

"These people, these people!"

"At night people turn evil," remarked the young man.

"What's he saying over there?"

"Who knows, he's always going on about something, that godless fellow."

"Let's push the wardrobe over on him, or turn him out of this house, turn him out right now!"

"Would you please stop it for once! This is hell!" The old man grumbled, the old woman grumbled in reply, the young man was quiet.

Every now and then someone would still grumble or spit out, but finally the room quieted down completely; the old woman fell asleep, the old man fidgeted one more time and then he, too, fell asleep. The young man once again started quickly buzzing like a bee, "Oh, Matylda!" but did not finish and fell asleep, too.

The pendulum continued ticking and stammering through the greasy air, just as before. Beside it, only the breathing sounds of the three sleepers could be heard. They intertwined but never came together.

2 Most of the House is Waking

The morning June sun had been illuminating the courtyard of the house for quite some time before people started waking up. The first footsteps echoed loudly from, it seemed, the vaulted ceiling despite the thundering of heavy wagons resounding from the street through the passageway and over the roof. Women, either bareheaded with their hair still unkempt, or with a headscarf pulled down low to protect their sleepy eyes from the sun, started emerging from their apartments one by one as though first waiting for the previous person to go their way. There were not many of them; they looked, though, like careless housemaids, their clothes were not even properly fastened, worn out shoes dragged on their feet, and they carried jugs either still empty or freshly filled up with milk.

Gradually, everything came to life. As curtains in the windows parted, many a window was opened and figures appeared, looking at the sky and Petřín Hill, then turning to remark upon the beautiful morning to the other occupants inside. They passed each other on the stairs and courtyard galleries wishing one another a good morning.

A tall man with a red blotchy face and dishevelled grey hair appeared in the side window on the second floor of the front part of the house leading to the street. He leaned heavily out of the window, bending so far forward that his opened shirt bared his large chest, which was – though it was June – still wrapped in flannel. He looked at the neighboring window with its curtains as yet drawn. Then he turned inside saying, "It's not seven yet."

All at once the neighboring window burst wide open. Another man, also tall but younger, appeared in it. His hair was black, carefully combed in a proper and fixed manner, hinting that it was probably the same down to the last strand of hair every single day. His face was round, closely shaved but, it seemed, expressionless. His body was concealed in an elegant, grey bathrobe, his hands holding a yellow silk kerchief which he used to wipe his gold-rimmed specs. He breathed on the glasses one more time, once more he wiped off the mist and then, putting the spectacles on, he turned completely towards us. His face, in the first moment nondescript, now acquired a more definitive character under the glasses, as always happens with the shortsighted. It was a good-natured face, his eyes now gazed kindly and quite merrily; yet we could read from every feature that his face had been looking at the world for well over forty long years. And if we were to look at it with even slightly expert eyes, we could be almost certain that it was the face of a bachelor. You can tell the face of a priest and a bachelor even in disguise.

The bachelor leaned out of the window over a snow white, finely embroidered pillow hanging to air. He looked up at the blue sky, glanced at the shining green Petřín Hill and his face reflected the joyful morning. "So beautiful – I've got to be getting up earlier," he whispered. In the next moment his gaze fell upon the second storey of the rear part of the house. A woman's clothes flashed by a closed, clean and transparent window there. The bachelor's smile brightened: "Of course, Josefinka is already in the kitchen," he whispered again. At the same time he moved his hand slightly and the diamond decorating the finger of his right hand flared up in a stream of splendid glow, which brought his attention back to his own person. He turned the ring a little so that the diamond would sit right above the middle of the knuckle, pulled down his elegant cuffs and with obvious fondness looked at his fleshy, gleaming white hands. "It won't hurt if they get some sun, it's healthy." Having whispered that, he raised his right hand to his nose as if to confirm his good health by smelling it.

A door on the opposite third storey leading to the courtyard gallery squeaked and a young woman of about eighteen came out. Morning personified! The young woman was of graceful, slender stature. Her dark, curly and rich hair spiraled from her forehead to the nape of her neck, bound only by a plain satin ribbon. Her face was round, her eyes light blue and frank, the skin on her rosy cheeks tender, her tiny lips almost dark red, her whole visage gave the most pleasant impression without ruling out a secret thought that the features are not altogether academically regular. But where would one find that irregularity given the overall pleasant impression? Certainly not in the lovely small ears, which were, to be sure, made to be kissed, even though they were adorned with only small, cheap, silver earrings. And apart from the earrings, there was no other ornamentation. An unbelievably thin black string coiled around her white neck, but the gem which it might have borne was hidden somewhere in the voluptuous bosom. Her dress, narrowly striped, was buttoned all the way up her neck. The simplicity of the colour and cut alone was enticing.

The young woman was carrying a brown jug covered with a tin lid in her hand.

"Good morning, Josefinka!" Called out a sonorous tenor.

"Good morning, Doctor!" answered Josefinka and looked over at the window with an affable smile.

"Whereabouts are you headed with the breakfast?"

"Down to Miss Žanýnka. She's ill so I'm bringing her a bit of beef broth. I kept it from yesterday."

"Žanýnka's ill? No wonder, her place must look like a prison! Wouldn't open her window year round and she keeps that ugly dog there to boot; it was barking and howling again all through the night. We should bring in a dog-catcher."

"No way," exclaimed Josefinka, "Miss would go crazy!"

"So what's wrong with her?"

"Old age," Josefinka answered sadly, on her way toward the spiral staircase.

"Such a good soul, Josefinka," muttered the doctor fixing his gaze on the end of the second floor staircase, and when the woman had passed through here, his gaze shifted down to the courtyard entrance, awaiting her there.

Josefinka crossed over the courtyard and approached a ground level door. She turned the handle but the door was locked. She rattled the handle, knocked on the door, but no one stirred inside. "Knock on the window!" the doctor advised from his window.

"That won't do, you've got to bang on the door, not knock, and she can't do it. Wait, I'll do it!" came from the steps of the passageway leading to the courtyard, and in two leaps down the stairs a young man of about twenty appeared, and in the blink of an eye was standing beside Josefinka. He was clad in light summer clothes with no hat or any other head covering. His hair was full of black locks, his face was sharp, his eye had a spark.

"Can you help me then, Mr. Bavor?" urged Josefinka.

"First, let's have a look under the lid," the young man teased and reached out toward Josefinka.

"Well, well, well," grumbled the doctor upstairs, but then fell silent when he saw the young woman deftly avoid the young man.

"I'll knock myself!"

But the young man was already standing beside the window and drumming on it with his finger. The piercing bark of a dog could be heard from inside and then once again everything became quiet. They waited a moment. But when there were no other signs of life, the young man took a few steps to the second window and started banging on the frame with all his might. The dog could be heard again, barking furiously and at great length, concluding with a piercing howl.

"Miss will tell us off for that!"

"Ah, so what!" responded the young man and went on banging again; then he put his ear to the frame and listened. He could hear only the whining howl of the dog.

The din brought about had already caused a disturbance throughout the whole house. In the window next to the doctor's, the tall man with the red blotchy face was looking out again, accompanied by the heads of two women, one older, the other younger. Josefinka's mother, a woman of tall stature, came out onto the opposite courtyard gallery on the second floor followed by Josefinka's older sister, a short, sick and hunch-backed woman, who now crept behind her.

Three people came out onto the courtyard gallery of the second floor: a half-dressed bald man, a woman that, too, was older and only half dressed, and finally there appeared a young woman of about twenty wearing only a shift with a shawl sloppily thrown over her, and her hair full of curl papers. Two other women, dressed only in plain clothes, were also coming down the steps of the passageway leading to the courtyard. The shorter of the two, a lively and agile person, called back into the passageway while coming down, "Márinka, stay in the taproom so no one gets in there!" The second, taller woman we recognize as the night time interpreter of dreams from the previous chapter. It is perhaps because her clean, white bonnet suits her well, or perhaps because all people are and seem to be meeker in the sunlight, that she now looks pleasant to us.

"What's going on here, Václav!" she says to the young man.

"It seems to me that Miss Žanýnka has died on us! I'll bang once more!" and he drummed with all his might.

"Well, you will need to get a locksmith, Mr. Bavor, but quick!" the doctor called from upstairs. "I'll get down there myself right away!"

The young Bavor had already left the courtyard. Questions and answers were crisscrossing from all sides, everybody was talking, but in, it seemed, sombre tones.

The doctor, who had just got completely dressed for a walk, came downstairs and as soon as he told the astounded Josefinka she did not need to go on holding the mug in her hand, young Bavor returned with a locksmith apprentice.

The lock was quickly torn away and the door no longer prevented entry. For a moment no one wanted to go in. Then Václav came round and bravely sprang inside, closely followed by the doctor, while the women thronged in the doorway.

The large room was dark, almost terrifying. The windows leading to the courtyard and Petřín Hill were thickly draped and did not allow in any light, only some shade. A stench hung in the old, musty air. Enormous black cobwebs heavy with dust hung from the ceiling, on the bare grey walls several dark pictures twined with age-old artificial flowers were covered in a thick layer of dust. There was no lack of implements, but everything was too old, too out-of-date, bearing no sign of having been used for years. Two pitiful, haggard, dried arms and a shrivelled, bald head could be seen in the low bed under dirty yellow covers. Lifeless open eyes stared glassily upwards. The old, ugly and shaggy black dog was running up and down from the head to the foot of the bed barking desperately at the approaching people.

"Hush, Azor!" spoke Václav in a stifled voice as if afraid to breathe in that air.

"I think she's dead, otherwise the dog wouldn't be howling like this," commented the doctor gloomily.

"Yes, she has gone to her final resting place! God forgive her sins and forgive us all our trespasses. Pray for us, Queen of Saints!" Mrs. Bavor stammered, a large tear running down her cheek. "When there's a funeral in the house followed shortly by a wedding, it means good luck for the bride," remarked the short innkeeper to the still astounded Josefinka.

She was deathly pale, then at once she started to blush, and grew pale again; thereupon she turned and left without uttering a word.

"First we have to get rid of the dog so that he won't bite us – he may already have the poison from the dead body in his teeth," stated the doctor, taking two steps back.

"He'll be out in no time," maintained Václav, approaching the raging keeper of the corpse. Although he knew all the faces before him, the dog was becoming increasingly infuriated. He jumped to the head of the bed and back with ear-splitting barking as Václav, trying to comfort him, approached. Václav stepped over to the bed, reached out with his left hand toward the covers and just as the dog jumped after it, grabbed him by the scruff of his neck with his right hand and hoisted him up in the air. The dog flailed about violently, but Václav held him in a firm grip.

"What to do with him?"

"Give me the key to our wood-shed, Mother, I'll put him in a box there in the meantime," and he was on the way out with the wailing dog.

"So the poor dog lady is dead, is she?" said a hoarse voice in the doorway. We recognize the speaker as the bald man we saw before at the first-floor courtyard gallery. The bald head is covered with an almost opalescent, shabby and faded top hat whose shape testifies to the many years it has been out of fashion. The fair hair on the temples is combed horizontally towards the eye. The skin on his face creases into great folds, as happens to people dried up from their former excessive obesity; as though each cheek was a bag emptied after a voyage. The body is square with a sunken chest and arms that dangle lifelessly.

"Yes, she is dead!"

"Well, then let's get her to a chapel quick so that we don't have a dead body in the house and end up with expenses!"

"You don't have to worry about that," said the doctor to the landlord, searching, in the meantime, through a box filled with papers lying on a table beside the bed. "The dead woman will pay for everything herself. It is clear that she had prepared everything for her death and that only yesterday she was still going through her papers. Here under this shaggy and greasy wig I found this letter addressed to Žanýnka indicating that she was a member of the St. Haštal Society and here's a book of the Strahov Venerable Society. She'll get money for her funeral, and she also has her requiem paid for."

"Poor dog lady, she managed all that on a pension of no more than eighty guilders a year; my son used to write quarterly receipts for her!" said Mrs. Bavor in admiration. It is clear that "dog lady" has long been to these folks but a mere historic term rather than an insult.

"She will be getting about fifty guilders, a nice pall, and a guilded tombstone," said the inn keeper.

"And what's in the other papers?" asked Václav curiously, having just returned.

"Nothing of value. Apparently private letters that are a couple of decades old," replied the doctor while scrutinizing them.

"Let me have a look at them, it could be interesting to read the memories of a spinster. I'll go up above the eaves with them and read them there. It's Monday, the entire house is washing their laundry and cooking peas at the same time; the smell of soap suds and peas makes it unbearable in the whole house except for on the roof. A novelist has to read everything and I want to be a novelist. I've got enough time, I have time off from the office until Thursday, right Landlord?"

"See that you don't lose any of these letters, return them all here!"

"But who will take care of everything?" asked the landlord. "You should take it up, Doctor! *Denn diese Leute kennen's nicht!*"

"If only my son wasn't in the same office with you, I'd show you *'kennensnicht!'*" muttered Mrs. Bavor to herself.

"Well, all right!" said the doctor kindly. "I personally will go to the Civil Registry, parish registry and the parsonnage, but you, Mr. Bavor, have to get a coroner right away; when he signs the official paper, please bring it to my office!"

Václav obligingly hurried away.

"Madam Innkeeper and I will wash and prepare the body. It will be our last service to her!"

"That's so good of you," the doctor praised them. "But I have to be going!"

"I'll go with you."

The men departed.

"What are you doing, Mrs. Bavor?"

"Pondering over the world."

"And what was the dream you had, neighbour?" the innkeeper kept asking. "You were going to tell me –"

"Oh, yes! That was a beautiful dream! I dreamt that I was visited by my late father, God bless him, he's been rotting for over twenty years now, and when Mother died before him, he found no rest and kept going to the cemetery every day until he died as well. He had an easy death. They loved each other like children! I can still see them both crying over us children. This was during the penury in the time of the French wars and they couldn't feed us."

"What was his name?"

"Nepomucký – number sixteen, after the martyr. So anyway, he's standing in front of me – in our store. And I want to say, 'What are you doing here, Father?' but he – all dressed in white – hands me an armful of sweet buns – twenty three, which means good luck – and he says, 'I've been conscripted, I have to go!' Army conscription is number eight, which means merriment. Then he turned and went away."

"That's sixty-one if he turned!"

"In all honesty, I wouldn't have realized that. So that makes 61, 23 and 8."

"And let's stake the full fifty guilders on these, since it was such a vivid dream, what do you say?"

"We could, I suppose."

"We'll win lots and then – after all, your Václav and our Márinka love each other, they'll make a marvellous match!"

3 In the Landlord's Family

It is time for me to give a more detailed account of the scene and the characters. With the latter, I depend on chance as it surfaces in the course of the day that has just begun; about the scene, however, I can already say that it is one of the quietest buildings in Malá Strana. It is an oddly built house, and even more of this kind can be found at the steepest slope of Ostruhová Street. The house is of rather considerable depth, its simple front façade looks out onto Ostruhová street, whereas the rear looks out onto the deep and dead end of Svatojánská Street. The slope makes the rear part, despite its two storeys, lower than the one storey front. The two parts are joined together not by the buildings, but rather by the windowless walls of the neighbouring buildings towering on both sides.

At the front there is a shop on the left and a tavern on the right. The second storey can be entered not from the dark passageway leading from the street, but rather via steps leading down to the courtyard, then to the right on the short courtyard gallery to a winding staircase, up to another short courtyard gallery, and from there to a small corridor. The entire floor between the street and the courtyard makes up only one apartment, occupied by a retired fiscal official with his wife and daughter. Josef Loukota, the 'doctor', actually a clerk without a doctor's degree, is renting a room from them and has to pass through the kitchen to reach his dwelling.

The spiral staircase leads even a little higher on to the attic. To the right and left of the staircase are wood-sheds. The courtyard is on a notable incline. On the ground floor of the rear part of the building are the living quarters of the late Miss Žanýnka, whom we are already familiar with, beside them are stairs to the basement, and beside them a spiral staircase leading to two more storeys and then on to the attic. Josefinka, together with her sick, older sister and their mother, the widow of an estate official, live on the second storey. Their apartment, which, too, takes up the whole of the rather small floor, has windows which look out onto the courtyard and Petřín Hill.

The landlord and his family, whom we had a chance to briefly encounter at the courtyard gallery, live on the first storey. Let us pay them a mannerly visit.

We enter the first room through the kitchen where we now see old Mrs. Bavor again, this time as the landlady's maid, washing laundry in a tub. The furnishings here are quite simple and out of date. To the left is a bed covered with a knitted bedspread, to the right a chest of drawers and a tall wardrobe, some chairs here and there, in the middle a round table covered with a faded and somewhat tattered table-cloth, in the windows a sewing table with a chair and footstool, on the wall between the windows a large mirror; the other walls, painted green, are bare. There is dust on the chest of drawers and the mirror frame, but that does not matter as it is the next room which is the parlour, and this is why Mrs. Bavor calls this first room simply the fine *Vorzimmer*. In the second, the furnishings consist of a piano, a sofa with a table in front of it around which are arranged about six chairs with white covers placed over them, and again a bed. The bed is made and a young girl, the landlord's second daughter, is lying around on it. The third room is the parents' bedroom.

The landlady is sitting at the first window of the first storey while her oldest daughter is sitting at the second one. The mother is still only half-dressed, her daughter is as yet wearing only a petticoat, even though it is almost eleven o'clock.

The landlady is a woman of sharp features, with a rather pinched face tapering off to a pointy chin. Wearing a pair of glasses, she is busy sewing a coarse fabric of sorts. Black marks painted on the fabric reveal it is military clothing. The young woman is, to put it in a nutshell, a blond of the most insipid kind. She takes after her mother, only the sharpness of her features is slightly moderated and her pointy chin has at least a hint of charming youthfulness. Her eyes are light blue, her hair does not seem very thick, but it is still rolled in paper curls. We now see that she is well over twenty years of age.

A basket with sewing notions sits on the window sill and a white, thin linen of sorts lies on the chair next to the young woman. A small ball of red thread lying on the linen suggests that the young woman has either already started marking the linen or else was about to do so. On the empty, little table, which wobbles anytime one moves, is an inkwell and beside it an open album with keepsake cards covered in writing; in front of the young woman is a white card with an old newspaper underneath it, and at hand on the window sill is an open notebook filled with poetry in German. The young woman undoubtedly wishes to conjure a bit of poetry onto the white card but we see she does not have her pen quite ready as yet; she is trying it out in the margins of the newspaper and has been using different ways of helping it along as displayed by her black, ink-stained lips.

Her mother looks up and over at her daughter, then shakes her head.

"You really want to work, don't you?"

"I'll get to it!"

"Were you in the kitchen when Loukota was looking in here this morning, Matylda? That's always his morning prayer!"

"What do I care about him, he can look as much as he wants!" answered Matylda in a sharp piercing voice.

"If you ask me, I'd sooner choose him over the lieutenant!"

"I wouldn't."

"He is also younger and he's kind, we've known him for years. He must have quite a bit of money saved up!"

"Oh, mother, you're so tedious!"

"And you're so dumb!"

"You're treating me like a towel to wipe your hands on. Why don't you just let me do what I want!"

"But I will, by all means, I am not going to get myself upset over you!" said her mother, putting her sewing away and going to the kitchen.

It was clear that the young woman was not going to get upset over it either. She calmly put the notebook of poetry in front of her, dipped her pen into the ink once again and started setting down letters one beside the other on the white card. She set them forth slowly and with apparent difficulty. Finally, the first line was finished, then after a considerable pause the second one, the third, and only after half an hour of painstaking effort did the whole stanza emerge on the paper. It read exactly like this:

Roszen verwelken, Mirthe bricht
Aber wahrer Freundschaft nicht;
Wahrer Freundschaft soll nicht brechen
Bis man einst von mir wird sprechen:
„Sie ist nicht mer."

Roses fade and myrtle snips
But not so of true friendships;
True friendships do not fade away
Until one says of me one day:
"She is no more."

The quatrain was written in Gothic script, the emphatic conclusion in Roman characters. Miss Matylda was gazing at her work of poetry in great contentment, she read the lines out to herself twice, the second time delivering the magnificent ending in a truly moving voice. Then she began signing her name. She managed to write the entire "M" and half an "a" when the pen gave out for lack of ink. She dipped her pen into the ink again, got her hand ready to sign, when a large round inkblot dripped beside the "a" she'd started.

On the alert, she raised the card and promptly licked the inkblot off.

Clearly, the inkblot did not disconcert her, and she would not start all over again because of it; she held the card against the light, waiting for the wet streak to dry up.

But then all at once, her mother stepped hastily from the kitchen into the room.

"The Bauers are coming over — and you are still not even dressed," she called right from the door. "Put something on, quick!"

"What are these dolts doing here again!" grumbled the young woman and put the still unsigned card under a blotter. She got up and went to the bed where a white bodice lay. The landlady in the meantime quickly picked up her sewing and hurled it into the other room behind the door.

"Valinka, don't get up now, someone is coming over," she commanded someone in the room, closing the door again.

Inquisitive female voices could already be heard in the kitchen. Miss Matylda ran to her place and took the ball of red thread, while the landlady, too, leapt over to the window and started to poke about in the sewing basket.

There was a knock at the door.

"Who is it?" asked the landlady.

The door opened and from behind it two women came into view who seemed, so as to appear well mannered, hesitant to enter.

"Ah — Mrs. Bauer — Matylda, look who's coming!"

"My goodness, that's marvellous!" cried the dutiful Miss Matylda, joyfully clapping her hands. "Aren't you a fine one, Marie, not visiting for so long!" and she warmly embraced the younger of the two women.

"We thought we would just drop in, Frau von Eber" explained the elder. "We were on our way up to see our uncle the canon and Marie would not stop harping on me, she so wanted to see Miss Matylda. Why haven't you paid us a visit for so long? That only shows who is really interested, we still come over here more often, but today we truly wanted only to drop in. I was telling Marie that we may not be coming at a good time, it's Monday, clothes washing day."

"Not in the least," refuted the landlady, "Why would the clothes being washed in the kitchen be in the way? Please sit down! Just look at the girls, they won't even let go of each other, they love one another so! Please don't smother the young lady, Matylda!"

She seated the ladies beside the window. The elder of the two very elegantly dressed ladies was about fifty, the younger about thirty, but her dried up face, which was very much like her mother's, despite the polite smile, was already bearing signs of unspeakable weariness. The only thing about her that showed any sign of life was a look of contempt in her eyes, which wandered over things as she inspected them.

They started a conversation, speaking now in Czech, now in German, as the wind blew.

"So long as there is no draught here," remarked the old lady, sitting down. "My teeth suffer greatly from rheumatism! The beautiful sky lured us out today, Miss Matylda, what a beautiful sky we have today!"

"I see that, it certainly is beautiful, elegant."

"Ever so elegant," agreed Miss Marie.

"You were already sewing today, Mrs. Eber?" asked Mrs. Bauer, picking up a piece of cut cloth. "But isn't this – material used for piecework?"

"Well, yes, it is – for piecework," Mrs. Bauer forced the words out of her throat, feeling instantly embarrassed. "Our maid, a poor woman, does piecework, and since she is doing my laundry, I was helping her out a bit. I feel sorry for her, she has to do so much stitching only to make about fifty kreutzers a week! These folks really have to toil away!"

"Yes, hapless people."

"And what are you doing, dear Matylda! You are embroidering monograms on clothes? Let me see, what letters are you making!" Miss Marie starts a conversation. "M – K? Ah, now I remember, I did hear you were getting married, then I must wish you luck! I heard it was Lieutenant Kořínek? I met him once at my uncle's, I know him a little – do you love him?"

Miss Matylda did not even blush, after all she did not need to in front of a girlfriend. "Yes, I made up my mind! I tell you, what is there to wait for! He is kind and he loves me, so why should I wait around only to become a spinster?"

"I didn't take good notice – but I believe he is blond – or could it be that his hair is already grey?" uttered Miss Marie innocently while fingering the pages of the scrapbook.

"Oh, but Kořínek is not that old!" said Matylda, blushing slightly. "It is only that he – as he told me – had always lived

in unhealthy apartments in Graz, lying with his head right beside a wet wall. He is honestly not that old!"

"Then the rascal is only putting it on! Men simply can not be trusted in anything!"

"Oh, he's a crafty one alright! Yesterday he sure made me laugh. I was teasing him that he smokes too much and asked him why. He told me that it was to get his lips used to hard work for when he really starts kissing. *Der ist witzig!*" Miss Marie's innocent chuckle showed she shared her friend's view of Mr. Kořínek's jest. "But why did he go over from a front-line regiment to a quartermaster corps if he is still such a lion?"

"They wanted to send him to Dalmatia, so he asked to be transferred from front-line service, due to the fact that his memory was failing him."

"And then he would not be able to find his way home from so far away, poor thing!" uttered Miss Marie compassionately.

"Every man has his flaws and Kořínek has money!" Miss Matylda quickly pointed out. "His father earned it in the French wars."

"Yes, I heard about that, he was buying broken legs or something like that back then – but this is something we girls don't understand!" added Miss Marie again quite innocently.

"Look at this, what a beautiful card he wrote for you," – and she went on to read the lines on the card in a low voice.

The card read:

Dein treues Herz und Tugend Pracht
Hat mich in Dich verlibt gemacht,
Mein Herz ist Dir von mir gegeben
Vergissmeinnicht in Todt und Leben.

W. Korzineck, Oberlieutenant

Your faithful heart and virtue true
Has made me fall in love with you,
My heart is yours to my last breath
Forget me not in life and death.

V. Kořínek, Lieutenant

"But why did he not write out his whole name, is it Wolfgang or Viktor or something like that?"

"Well – his name is actually Václav, but he doesn't like it. He says that every time there was a holy procession he'd think of getting rechristened."

"And here you have a notebook full of poetry!"

"Kořínek lent it to me."

"I see, so that you can write some of it out for him, too. That's nice! Momma, shouldn't we set out yet?"

The mothers were engaged in a conversation about domestic matters. "You are right, we'll be on our way! It's a pity we won't see Herr Eber, but so it goes since he is in his office! But where is my little angel, my dear Valinka, isn't she home?"

"She is, but she's still in bed. I let her sleep in this morning, it's supposed to be good for the voice! Valinka is going to be a singer, you see, everybody's amazed by her. She's a little hellion when it comes to music, there is smoke rising out of the piano when she gets up from it!"

"But I must give my little angel a hug, I can't leave without a kiss! She's here in the next room, isn't she?" and Mrs. Bauer approached the door to the second room.

"But our beds are not even made up there yet!" protested the lady of the house.

"Come now, Mrs Eber, between you and me! It's no different at our place, I'm telling you!" and she was already at the door. The others had no choice but to follow.

Mrs. Bauer set her eyes upon the pile of piecework. A faint smile crossed her thin face, yet she didn't say a word, but walked quickly to the bed.

"Leave me alone – I don't want to!" Valinka resisted the embrace.

"What's that, now, behave yourself!" her mother scolded her. "But there's something I've just remembered! We have a little recital here on Thursday, why don't you join us, too, Madame Bauer! Matylda, why don't you convince Miss Marie to come on Thursday for certain!"

"We will come, we will come to admire our little angel," promised Mrs. Bauer kindly.

The parlour was as large as the kitchen and the first room together, thus it also had two windows facing the courtyard. The young women, hand in hand, approached one of them.

They saw young Bavor as he was just coming from Žanýnka's apartment, hastening with a handful of pages toward the spiral staircase.

"Who is that?" asked Miss Marie.

"That's our 'starling', the son of our maid, the grocer's wife! But he's so swollen-headed, he even carries his coat over his arm!"

"His name is Starling?"

"No, it's Bavor, but we call him 'starling'. We once had a starling which flew away and Papa thought he saw it on the roof. But when he climbed up, it turned out to be not a starling but rather the bottom corner of young Bavor's jacket; Bavor was always up on the roof studying. Now he's going up there again, look!"

"He is a student, then?"

"No, now he's in Papa's office, but Papa says that nothing will become of him, that he would do best to jump off the bridge like St. Jan Nepomucký."

"So girls, it's time to say goodbye to each other, Marie," called Mrs. Bauer.

The young women started embracing each other. It took a while before they'd kissed one another enough, it took a while before they all finally made their way through the room, the kitchen and all the way to the staircase, while paying endless compliments.

The landlady remained standing at the courtyard gallery with Miss Matylda.

"Did you hear that, Matylda, how afraid she was of rheumatism?" asked the landlady as Mrs. and Miss Bauer descended from the second storey onto the courtyard. "And she probably doesn't have a single real tooth in her mouth!"

"No way, her maid always washes her teeth after lunch together with the dishes!"

Mrs. Bauer turned back before the passageway and once again motioned in a kind, farewell gesture. Miss Marie blew Miss Matylda a few more fluttering kisses. Then they disappeared in the dark passageway.

"God only knows how many times Matylda has embroidered monograms on shirts and linens, always for a different bridegroom, and how many times she has been taking up the stitches again," remarked Miss Marie while straightening out her cape. "And perhaps she will be forever unstitching!"

"But what about Kořínek? Didn't uncle once talk to you about him? What do you think of him?"

"Hmmm! – well!" uttered Miss Marie and swung out onto the street.

4 Lyrical Monologue

The morning came and went and it was now the evening of the first day. It's evening and the setting is like from an old Russian song, "the moon in the sky – the moon in the chamber." High above, the full moon making its way across the sky is so bright that the stars around it fade away and only those that are a world away from it begin timidly to shine again. The moon proudly spreads its glowing coat across the land, covering the water of the rivers and the greenery around, the wide open fields as well as the outstretched city, drags it through the squares and streets, wherever it can find space, and when it finds an open window of a room somewhere, throws the bottom corner of its golden coat there, too.

It drifted through an open window to the doctor's meticulously tidied, clean, even elegant room, and all alone it was the master of the house there for a long time and liked it there. It poured over the plants on the pedestal near the window, so they looked as if covered by a silver hoarfrost, it lay down on the dazzling white bed, making it appear even whiter, it sat down in a comfortable chair and shone on various writing implements on the desk, and it even stretched out all over the carpet.

It remained this way for quite a long time, well into the night. Finally, the click of the handle could be heard, the door gave a sleepy squeak and the owner of the place entered.

The doctor put his cane into a stand beside the door, hung his straw hat on it and then rubbed his hands together. "Well, look at that," he muttered in a stifled voice, "We have a visitor! Welcome Mr. Moon, have you already come for Whitsun? Is everyone at home doing all right? Well – damned knee!" he muttered in a louder voice, bent down and rubbed his knee. His face, turned into the moonlight, was half frowning, half smiling.

He stood up again and began to take off his coat. As he was opening the closet to hang up his coat, he muttered again, this time, though, singing to himself: "Doctor Bartolo – Doctor Bartolo – Doctor Bartolo – lolo – lo – Was that an E or an F – yes, it was an F – Bartololo – lolo – lolo –." In the meantime he took his grey housecoat off the stand, put it on, tied the red silk cord around himself and walked freely to the open window, still loloing."

"Ah, Josefinka is surely already asleep – bye, sweetie, and beautiful dreams to you! She is so lovely – and so kind-hearted!" He suddenly bent forward and rubbed his knee, but this time didn't swear. He leaned out over the window-sill. "Their apartment is large enough and they don't even need it now. We'll stay there – only add some new furnishings! We will hold Mother and ill Katuška dear, they are good people. She has nobody else anyhow, that Bavarian cousin will be the best man, Josefinka has got to have a best man at the wedding, it's a matter of course, my love! We will do it on the sly – Bartololollo – How is it that I can't get the doctor of Seville out of my head, why is that! Bartolo – Bartolo – I'm not that old and I'm well-preserved, quite well-preserved, no doubt about that! I'm no *periculum in Morea*. I need not fear that I won't get any handsomer than now. It will be a new way of life for me, I will be happy and when you are happy, you become young again." He looked at the round moon. "I wonder if my sweetie is dreaming anything right now! Probably not, a child like her would be sound asleep. If only I could whisper to her what to dream!"

He turned back and took down his guitar from the wall above the pedestal. He stood back in the window with it and tried a few chords. A dog's hollow howl could be heard down in the courtyard.

"Ah, Azor somehow got away from them!" said the doctor and leaned out the window. "Azor – hush, be a good dog!" The dog fell silent. "I shouldn't aggravate the poor thing," said the doctor to himself then, hung his guitar back up, closed the window and pulled the curtains shut.

He went to the desk and lit a candle. Then he sat down. When alone the doctor always talked to himself in a low voice. And now he continued right where he had left off.

"I'm not young enough anymore to be too foolish. At my age one has to get this over with quickly, but not too quickly, not without it being poetic. I have a good plan – damned knee, I certainly must have bumped it all right!" He opened the housecoat and inspected his light long johns. The long johns were torn over the right knee.

"New long johns!" he lamented sullenly. "That's what you get for being considerate. They were standing on the left side of the passageway – it was definitely Václav and Márinka, who else – I carefully passed them by, steering to the right and bumped myself against the mangle! Damned Václav! But I have to talk him out of this affair, he's still only a practicant, where would this end! I feel sorry for him, he is talented, to give credit where it is due, and it would be best if he could finish his studies. But that's hard without having any means of support. I also have to talk him out of his poetry writing, it doesn't get anyone anywhere, he should hold on to his office work since he's got his foot in the door! When he comes back to hear my opinion, I'll tell him to throw it all away since it's worthless."

He took a thick notebook from the desk and started browsing through it. The notebook had bookmarks in it and he opened it at the first one.

"My plan is ready," he continued talking to himself, "I need poems but can't write them myself and these will actually serve me quite well. If I didn't take them from here, I'd take them from elsewhere, and so what? Josefinka won't learn about it and neither will he since he will throw them away on my advice. Tomorrow then, let me send the first one, for the time being anonymously, she will surely infer it anyway! This will be the first one!"

He went on to read from the notebook:

Thou art a mountain vista fair,
Its youthful springtime fresh!
Thy hair the deep, dark wood of dreams,
Thine eyes the dance of lively streams,
Thy lips, thy cheeks, buds I admire,
Thy voice doth sing the nightingale song –
Thou art thyself the world entire,
Thou art a mountain vista fair,
Now cloudy and now bright,

Thou art a mountain vista fair,
Beauty in the poet's sight!
Oh tell me if my song doth move
Thee to receive me in thy heart,
Or like the mountain vista thou,
Art stone that begs me to depart!?

"What a fellow! This is just like the mountains back home, and I know that he has never set foot anywhere near a mountainous landscape, not at all! 'Dreams – streams,' that's good! 'Thy voice doth sing the nightingale song' – that may be too much, though! I know what, I'll underline it with a thick line: 'Beauty in the poet's sight' – meaning only for me, for one person. Girls' passions are easily stirred by poetry! – And in a week there will be another bomb, perhaps already a signed one, depending on how things turn out! This will be the second one!"

And he read on:

Thy dark skin, thy raven hair,
Have sown a gloomy dream my way,
Thy fiery eyes, thy youthful voice,
Make of my night a burning day!

Oh, my dark sun!
Pray tell, if thou wilt in the dark of night
Be my bright, glowing light?

Oh, my dark moon!
Pray tell, if thou wilt in the heat of day
My true companion stay?

"He really knows how to give it what it takes, heh, heh! He can score with any girl he wants! But perhaps he wrote it for a Jewish woman, Josefinka is not so dark! – But that doesn't matter, she won't notice that, what's important is that she's like a sun and that it sounds nice. This poem will score with her! Full of burning heat! – But if she is then still implacable, a third one will do the trick, and then I can really get down to business!"

He turned a few pages and read on:

I'd fire a shot right through my heart,
And in an instant die!
Were I not sure that in my breast
You'd breathe your final sigh.

I'd go through pain and suffering,
Set off on that dark journey!
Were I not sure you're in my heart,
And so would have have to join me!

"There's something fascinating about it, shooting oneself!
A girl won't resist when her lover threatens to shoot himself. In any case, let's give Josefinka also a third pill. It will
make her love strong – but suddenly I feel half asleep – I have
to get to bed – yes, to bed!"

With a big yawn he started taking his clothes off.

"The best part is still: 'you're in my heart and so would
have to join me,'" he muttered while undressing himself, and
in his pedantically tidy way, folded his clothes over a chair
beside the bed. "It means he wants to say that he has her
locked in his heart and if he shot himself, he would at the
same time hit her since she's there, heh, heh, that's as plain
as the nose on one's face!"

"In my heart – it's warm today, I don't need slippers," he
went on muttering while taking off his shoes. He turned
back the covers, blew out the candle and lay down.

Once in bed, he let out a contented sigh.

"Bartolo – – oh dear! – In my – but so would have to join
me – and –". And he fell asleep.

Azor let out a howl down in the courtyard. In a while his
scratching on Žanýnka's door could be heard. As if unable to
overcome his sorrow and yet afraid to wake someone up, the
dog went on crying out his muffled howls all night.

5 "A Bachelor is a Lucky Fellow"
an old saying

The fiscal official who is renting a room to the doctor is called Lakmus. He has been living in Prague for only about three years and he inherited the tenant from the apartment's former resident.

Soon after he moved into our quiet house, all the other occupants knew that the Lakmus family had saved up a fortune, that they were receiving a comfortable pension, an allowance in kind, and they regarded them with respect. But there was not much contact with them. Mrs. Lakmus, the head of the family, kept to herself. Though she readily obliged everybody, willingly paying the rent in advance any time the landlord asked, lending others flour or butter from her own supplies any time they needed, answering their greetings without hesitation, even greeting them first, she nevertheless never spoke to them at great length. This is not to say, however, that she was taciturn, as evidence of her oratorical disposition could be heard resonating now and then from the open windows through the whole floor.

Mrs. Lakmus, though she was over forty years of age, was still quite lively. Her plump figure was still fresh, her gleaming face still free of any wrinkles, her eye had a cheerful spark, in short, she looked like a merry widow, even though her daughter had reached marrying age some time ago now. Miss Klára, a little over twenty, did not look like her. She was lanky, lacking her mother's pleasant round shape; but her light blue eyes were a good match for her full flaxen hair, and her red elongated cheeks were still reddish, reminiscent of healthy country living. Miss Klára was even more standoffish than her mother; the landlords' daughter, Miss Matylda, has therefore not been seeking friendship with her for some time now.

Mr. Lakmus was seldom seen anywhere else but in the window. His leg was badly ailing and he required constant care at home. Scarcely once in several months would he ever limp out of the house; he spent all his time at home either looking out the window onto the street or tending to himself on the chesterfield, wrapped in flannel and wet clothes. It was said that he drank a lot of wine and his blotchy face did not contradict this.

It was already noon on the second day of our story when Mr. Lakmus painstakingly lifted himself up out of the chair by the window over the street, in which he always spent his morning hours, and he was now slowly heading for the sofa. Here he sat down again, stretched his leg out on the sofa and with a somewhat impatient sigh looked at the large, loudly ticking clock set behind glass, which, like all the other furnishings was not new, yet still testified to considerable expense. The hand showed several minutes before twelve.

His gaze travelled from the clock to Klára, who was busy diligently sewing at the other window. "You haven't even made me soup today!" he said with a wry smile intending only a reminder rather than a reproof.

The door suddenly opened and Miss Klára looked up as Mrs. Lakmus entered the room carrying a steaming mug on a plate. Mr. Lakmus' face lit up.

"Klára, go in the kitchen and start making the souffle!" ordered her mother. "And be careful with it so the doctor doesn't laugh at you!"

Klára left. "I've made you wine soup today, you must be tired of beef soups by now, my dear hubby," said Mrs. Lakmus kindly and put the plate in front of her husband. Mr. Lakmus looked up and gazed at his wife somewhat mistrustfully, as though suspicious of her frugality. However, he was clearly prepared to be submissive since he immediately abandoned his mistrust and began to sip the delicacy offered to him.

Mrs. Lakmus took a chair and put it beside her husband's chesterfield. She sat down, placed her hands on the table and fixed her eyes on her husband.

"Tell me, husband, what are we going to do with Klára?"

"With Klára! – Well, what should we do with her?" answered Mr. Lakmus, sipping his soup.

"The girl is all infatuated and what's that good for? She's all crazy about Loukota, you know ..."

"She hasn't told me anything!"

"What is she going to be telling you, but she tells me everything, she is honest with me. Last night I had to pull her out of the kitchen. Apparently she heard the doctor say something so wonderful there, that she would not go away. I'm telling you, the girl is all infatuated and what's the good of that? She should marry him, don't you think?"

With the back of his hand, Mr. Lakmus wiped off the beads of perspiration planted on his forehead by the powerful soup. "He's too old for her," he remarked after a while.

"Too old! You were not a youth either and I still married you!"

Her husband did not breathe a word.

"He's still well preserved, in good health, doesn't even look old and isn't. We know him, I would choose him rather than some fop, especially now that she's been so difficult lately. You know he has some few thousand guilders saved up and he is able to provide for a wife, so why not give our daughter to him – isn't that right – why don't you say something?"

"But who knows if he wants her ..." Mr. Lakmus daringly pointed out.

"Well, of course, we can't force her upon him if he's not interested," his wife said annoyed. "Wouldn't that be something! I'll have a word with him – Klára is pretty – he always smiles at her, she keeps his little room tidy and he's so keen on tidiness – I believe he would miss her, I mean he only lacks confidence since he is no longer – well in the prime of his life. Of course, that's how it is – but I'll take care of things!" She nodded in satisfaction. At once she stopped nodding and tilted her head toward the door. "Indeed," she said then. "He's already home today – unusually early! He was speaking to Klára in the kitchen, but has already gone to his room. I must to the kitchen – to take care of everything at once!"

Mrs. Lakmus ran into the kitchen. Miss Klára was standing at the kitchen table working dough in a bowl. Her mother approached her and took her head into her hands turning her face toward herself. "You're turning red as a rose," she said softly. "And you're all trembling – oh my! But don't you worry, everything's going to be all right."

She looked in the small mirror on the wall, adjusted her bonnet, pulled down her sleeves and walked up to the doctor's door. She knocked. Nothing could be heard from inside. She knocked again, this time more vigorously.

The doctor could hardly bear being in the office today. He was distracted, almost grumpy, trembling with a restlessness half pleasant, half embarrassing. He was trembling with a poetic feeling of sorts, and as everyone who has ever experienced this feeling knows, it does not allow for work as outlined on the drawing board of everyday life. Some kind of unclear thought keeps creeping back and forth in our brain like a caterpillar, tickling and scratching, first agitating one nerve, a second one, then a third, until the whole nervous system is agitated. There is no other way but to give up all work, focus our entire attention on that thought until it finally settles down and wraps itself into a solid cocoon. And if the sun of one's fantasy is warm enough, the cocoon bursts and into the world flies a butterfly – a poem.

The doctor's butterfly glittering in the colours of a "mountain vista fair" flew out right away in the morning. He had set it forth in ink on a sheet of pink paper, which he slipped into an envelope, sealed with a scented sealing-stick and entrusted to the postal service. The agitation did not come until later, yet it grew the way love does later in life, until finally it drove him away from the office.

He slowly dawdled home. Upon entering the courtyard from the passageway, he omitted looking up at Josefinka's windows as was his old habit. When entering the Lakmus' kitchen with strangely uncertain steps, he felt as if he had just escaped some danger. He sighed with relief, his blood started to circulate more freely and he spoke to Klára pleasantly as never before. But he did not stay long and continued directly on to his room.

He closed the door. His head tilted to his chest. As if unawares, he slipped out of the right sleeve of his jacket, then became absorbed in thought. He was involuntarily driven to the window. He did not know when the letter he'd sent in the morning would be delivered and whether Josefinka would already have received it or not. As if afraid of some punishment, he remained standing about three steps away from the window, looking to the other side through the gap between the curtain and the window frame. Suddenly he started – a mailman had just entered the opposite gallery.

He leapt back when he suddenly heard knocking on the door. "Come in," he forced the words out of his throat and started blushing like a French rose.

The door opened and Mrs. Lakmus appeared in it. The doctor tried quickly to catch the sleeve he had taken off and a forced smile danced its twisted whirl across his face.

"I'm not disturbing you, Doctor, am I?" asked Mrs. Lakmus, closing the door behind her.

"Not at all – you are most cordially welcome my dear lady," stuttered the doctor as he caught his dangling sleeve.

"You've come home so early today, Doctor, that's so unusual – I hope you're not ill."

"How is that, dear lady?" he asked oafishly still, lost in his emotional insecurity.

"Oh, my –," the lady went up to him and put her hand on his forehead, "If you don't mind; no, Doctor, something is really wrong with you. You are glowing like a young maiden, perhaps ..."

"I ran, I always run – I do, dear lady –," stuttered the doctor.

"How about a compress?"

"Oh, no, no, I'm all right, quite all right! But please do take a seat, my dear lady, just so that ...," the doctor bade Mrs. Lakmus, leading her to a chair. Mrs. Lakmus sat down while the doctor took the seat opposite her.

"You keep calling me 'my dear lady' as if I was truly your dear one," flirted the woman with a smile that would surprise the doctor any other time. "Well, if it was not for my husband – my husband, though, is truly a good soul – well, you never know! But this way I have to let others, younger ones, have you," she continued making merry.

The doctor smiled a little but, since he did not know what to say, remained silent.

"Wouldn't you agree, Doctor, that it's wonderful when one has someone to call 'my dear'?"

"Well, yes – of course – when two hearts yearn for each other – especially in the spring ...," the doctor made an effort.

"But look at the way you talk today – you rascal! Who could blame you if you were considering tying the knot! You are in the prime of life, sound as a bell, you've been frugal ..." The doctor was on tenterhooks. He thought Mrs. Lakmus knew everything about his secret love, about Josefinka, about the poem. He suddenly gathered courage and pulled himself together. "Then at least I can tell myself that I've been careful with both health and money, too," he commended himself.

"Quite so," approved Mrs. Lakmus. "You can certainly consider finding a woman quite young!"

"Well, I wouldn't take an old one, she would already be moulded, and couldn't be formed any other way than the way she already was," remarked the doctor cautiously. "But I would only consider such a young woman that was kind, obedient, soft, and could still wholly adapt to me ..."

"By all means," agreed Mrs. Lakmus, "You should consider only such a woman! But tell me – and I mean heart to heart – as honestly as if you were talking to the mother whose daughter you want," – and she took the doctor by the hand and looked deeply into his eyes – "Tell me, haven't you been considering it?"

"Well, since the cat is out of the bag, why be ashamed!" confessed the doctor sincerely. "Yes!"

"But that's what I was telling my husband!" Mrs. Lakmus clasped her hands in glee.

"How did – Mr. Lakmus –"

"It is so! He said, 'who knows if he wants her', fancy that!"

"Why wouldn't I want her?"

"I knew it all along! You rascal, fixing this going on behind the mother's back!"

"The mother's back? Why would I, when I thought that nobody knows anything, not even the daughter!"

"The daughter didn't know but mothers can see everything! The girl was so unhappy! All confused; during the day she speaks about nothing but you, during the night she talks in her sleep, I'm telling you I was young once myself, but I've never seen anything like it!"

The doctor's mouth fell open in amazement. His eyes revealed ignorance, embarrassment and a smug smile.

"Well, now that worked out well," remarked Mrs. Lakmus again. "First I didn't want a tenant, but now I'm glad, because Klára will be so happy."

"Miss Klára ...?" marveled the doctor, rising from the chair.

"As I said, she's completely infatuated! But you'd better not wait around with the wedding; you live with us, people would talk, so why hesitate! We know you, you know us – you can see that we have been blessed with a comfortable life, so everyone will benefit."

"I beg your pardon," stuttered the doctor anew, and paced up and down taking long strides, "but I thought that Miss Klára was seeing some official?"

"She was but she is not seeing him anymore. He got married to a miller's widow. And do you think she grieved his loss? God forbid, she was already in love with you and it was as if she'd become a different woman! Even though I told her: 'Forget it, the doctor won't be interested in a woman that has been kissed so many times before', but she wouldn't hear of it! But as you know, one lover is no lover!"

The doctor did not know what to do, but Mrs. Lakmus went on herself in an instant.

"Let's not put it off, shall we? You've got all your papers in order anyway, don't you? Such a tidy gentleman!"

The doctor nodded. Mrs. Lakmus interpreted that in her own way. "So why don't you take care of all the documents, you're good at that. Today you'll dine with us, won't you?"

"No, no!" blurted out the doctor forcefully. "Just here – actually!"

"You're still like a young man," smiled the contented mother-in-law. "Klára won't be able to eat a thing, when I tell her all this!"

"For heaven's sake don't tell her anything, nothing at all, I beg you," implored the doctor frantically.

Mrs. Lakmus found it all quite amusing. "If there were no people with more common sense around you, I would like to see how you two would ever carry anything through. So please do have your papers ready, Doctor. Is there anything else you'd like?"

"No!"

"Bye for now then, Doctor!"

"So long!"

The doctor stood frozen in the middle of the room for a long time.

At last he let out a sigh of relief and shook his head. "Now what do you think of that!" he grumbled fiercely. "Yes, I will have my papers arranged, dear unexpected mother-in-law, but not for your daughter, would-be mother-in-law! – – There's no other way but to make haste! Tomorrow I'll put forth the second poem, the day after tomorrow the third, and the following day – no that's Friday, who knows what could happen – then straight away the day after tomorrow I will go courting! And then quickly get another apartment, or for God's sake then I really will have something to look forward to when coming or going – and then–"

He did not finish his words. The door opened and Mrs. Lakmus entered accompanied by the maidservant, carrying a silver service.

"I put out the silver service for you, Doctor, why should we hide our silver!" She approached the doctor, put her hand on his shoulder and whispered in a low voice, "You know, I did tell Klára, after all!"

6 Manuscript and Clouds

This chapter begins the very moment the previous one ended, when Mr. Eber, the landlord, returns home from the office. The landlady, busy stoking the fire in the kitchen stove, almost got a fright by her husband's arrival. Usually, he came home close to three o'clock in the afternoon, but today he was here already after twelve, and on top of that, he looked strange in a way that she had not seen him for a long time. Everything about him was different compared to the morning, beginning with the shabby top hat which was pressed down almost all the way to the thick bristly eyebrows, casting shadows over the wilted folds of his once corpulent cheeks. His hair, combed straight before, now spiked out from underneath the top hat; his eyes, normally indifferent, were apparently trying to communicate something, his wide mouth was tightly closed so his chin stood a bit higher, his sunken chest was somewhat thrust out, and his right hand held a long scroll of sorts horizontally, while his left arm swayed like the arm of a marionette when the puppet master for a moment does not know what to do with it.

The landlady took one look at him, a thought flashed through her mind in an instant, and her sharp face grew longer.

"I hope they didn't let you go at the office," she said in a voice that suddenly became hoarse. Her husband gestured with his head a little as if such a query offended him in the most annoying way. "Go get that Bavor woman!" said he in darkening tones.

The landlady would hardly withstand such an ambiguous answer any other time, but her husband's unusual appearance had an impact on her; besides, there was no time for any bitterness to evolve. She looked out the window. "She's just on her way over here," she said as she saw Mrs. Bavor coming down into the courtyard.

Mr. Eber entered the room. He advanced towards the table in the middle and remained standing there. He merely fixed his eyes on the table since they had to be looking somewhere, he did not take off his hat, neither did he put the scroll down – it was obvious that he was set upon something he neither would nor could let go of.

Miss Matylda looked at her father in surprise. At last she exploded into roaring laughter. "But Papa," she cried. "You look like a strained pigeon that stuffed itself with vetch!"

The landlord made only the slightest movement, yet it revealed the gravest dissatisfaction.

All at once the door opened and the landlady entered followed by Mrs. Bavor.

"Here she is – so go ahead and tell her whatever it is you wanted!" stated the landlady.

The landlord half turned towards the entrant. He set his eyes on the floor, his mouth opened and he started to speak in a solemnly monotonous voice. "I am very sorry Mrs. Bavor, but it can't be helped – there is nothing that I could do about it! Your son has got himself into deep trouble! Yes, deep trouble! He's thoughtless, careless, everything! Now he's in trouble! He had the guts to write something about the whole office, something shameful about all of us, even the president! Yes! And he wrote it in the office and had it in his drawer there, and now that he took time off he simply left it lying there, and they found it there; he's thoughtless, he didn't even take the key out. So they started reading it, it's in Czech, and such terrible writing. The president knows my Czech is the best, so he gave the disgraceful thing to me to report on. There are supposed to be scandalous things in it; oh, I don't know, but you may expect even the worst, you are his mother, so I thought it my duty to let you know, you should be prepared for anything! Now I'll have my wife bring me a wash-basin and fresh drinking water into my room and not let anyone in unless it's someone from the office, don't even call me for dinner, I'll come myself. Good day to you, Madam!"

Mrs. Bavor was pale; her lips quivered, her eyes turned red. "Good God, I beg you my dear sir, we are poor people –" she uttered a piercing cry.

The landlord interrupted her with a dismissive gesture. "I neither can nor am allowed to do anything about it. It's too late and everything is past hope! Duty is duty, and justice has to be done! That would really be something if lads like that – well, I'm going now."

He took a few short restrained steps and disappeared into the next room.

After closing the door behind himself with an air of solemnity, he swayed right and left, and only then did he take off his hat. He stepped up to the desk and placed the scroll on it carefully as if afraid it might break.

Normally, he just came home and undid his clothes to feel comfortable; this time he ceremoniously adjusted his apparel in front of the mirror. Then he examined all his pens, dusted the blotter, and shifted his chair around before seating himself.

When he finally took the scroll in his hand to unwrap it, he raised his eyebrows to the top of his forehead and his eyes cautiously scrutinized every fold of the paper.

7 Fragments of the Practicant's Notes

I am finished with my work, there's nothing left to do! I can only hand it in tomorrow, though, after all, I got an earful for my first assignment; supposedly it couldn't possibly have been done properly, but only haphazardly since I'd finished it so soon.

I will write little feuilletons about the office, images of everyday life, snapshots and biographies of these gentlemen, my colleagues and supervisors, flashes of bureaucratic life and little ditties from a practicant. An English satirist wrote a travelogue about a journey which took place at his own desk; I will travel farther than that, I will turn to all the neighbouring desks, take a trip across our president's empire and describe the land and the people. I only hope the people will provide an opportunity for juicy satire! And why wouldn't they? Only people completely wise or completely dull are not fit for satire; in the one case it would make you cry and in the other it would have to resort to lofty perspectives and then turn into the ill-natured argument that in the face of eternity everything we do is ludicrous.

I certainly won't need any esoteric philosophy for that sleek junior clerk over there, a small mirror, like the one he routinely stares into, will do. He is nice to me, on my first day I was asking someone who that "handsome" gentleman was, and he overheard it. But the others – how diligently they write, how they work! What faces, what heads, what eyes! These wouldn't even be fitting for anyone but a clerk, it is as if they do everything by the book!

Their faces show that their "mental" work does not exert them, and that not a single thought of theirs would ever rise above bureaucratic matters. It apparently doesn't matter to them whether they labour over files or over crops like plough horses. Step by step, everything scrupulously by the book! But perhaps among those "mental" plough horses some Trojan horses can still be found: wood on the outside and Greeks on the inside. Let's open them up!

Only the supervisor is taking it easy and reading a newspaper.

Now he's putting it away ...

* * *

What a look he gave me when I asked him if I could borrow his newspaper to read, too! He didn't say a word and I was burning red and before I could sit back at my desk, my eyes burned with tears of shame. I couldn't see anything for the tears but I felt all those present open their mouths in amazement over the practicant's boldness!

* * *

I wish I was back in school with all the prospects of everything in the world and at the same time nothing! Here my prospects are narrowing and I really have no idea how high I can rise!

The first day they tested me for style and asked me to describe what I felt when I looked at a steam engine. I hitched up Pegasus to the engine and boldly went riding through the empire of human progress. The president, they say, stood there shaking his head and remarked on what a strange character I was.

Before even speaking to anyone I had already overheard them calling me an "incendiary". It won't be easy that's for sure! I wish I was back in school. But that is not to be.

The air here! Prometheus' soil was supposed to have smelled of human flesh, these people here smell of soil, but bone dry.

What dreadful people! They're about where I was as a little boy still throwing stones at starlings and pulling rats by their legs. Then I read Robinson Crusoe in German and thought that *Insel* meaning 'island' was the same as *Insicht*, which of course means 'insight', and I still liked it. The people here hold such a simple view of the world, and yet they like that world. They consider ideas a state monopoly like salt or tobacco. What was I thinking expecting a Trojan horse; wood on the outside, wood on the inside, you can bang on it as much as you want, there's still nothing but wood!

Yesterday I told them that Parisian ladies wear feathers from Brazilian apes, the day before I told them that the archbishop's ceremonial carriage was modelled on St. Elijah's chariot, tomorrow I'll cut off some hair from Azor's tail and tell them it's the hair that Isis tore out of her head when Osiris died.

They consider me greatly learned and like to talk to me. But they dare not make a sound in the presence of the boss, unless he makes a joke, whereupon a general exercise in laughter begins. When the boss steps out of the room though, a general shuffle resumes and each face broadens and all the stooped backs straighten up. It's a part of their daily routine that they secretly pull out their watches to see if the ever-punctual boss isn't about to step out.

* * *

My reputation as a learned man continues to spread all the while. I was able to read a Serb business letter written in Cyrillic script, which astounded them. The superintendent from Department Five patted me on the back in passing and said, "Anything can be useful at some point, but hold on to practical things!" This boss enjoys the reputation of being a skillful writer. He apparently even published a book, heelology, I believe, meaning a manual for the efficient use of foot rags.

* * *

I'll never see anything like this again!

The president came to our department for some document or other. He stood with one foot on the ladder, and when he retreated again, he stepped on the foot of Mr. Hlaváček. Out of reverence, that old ass didn't want to tell the president that he was standing on his foot. He seemed like a second Laocoon; his face bore an expression of pain and yet the mandatory academic smile of a law clerk remained engraved on it. Finally, the president noticed that someone was standing directly behind him; he wanted to put down that unmannerly person, but noted that underneath him was not the end of a pack of documents but rather someone else's affronted foot. "Oh, pardon me!" he said with a gracious smile. Mr. Hlaváček, though, limped towards his desk, smiling in his great pain, a true model for a noble and touching sculpture. The others surely envied him – who knows if he couldn't benefit from this at some point.

* * *

The president kindly asked me whether I had any sisters. I understood exactly that old bachelor's question – just you wait, you will pay for that question dearly! After all, I know, honourable president, where you indulge in love to your heart's content; the handsomest clerk of all told me! She is supposed to be really beautiful, this lover of yours; the younger I am than you are, the more beautiful she will be to me. When I finally get to see her! And if she's not for me, then she'll surely be for the clerk, who practically sees himself as handsome as Narcissus. Something is sure to happen!

* * *

The president kindly called us all in to his office. There were many of us small fry facing the bosses who were standing in a semi-circle. They were whispering among themselves while the rest of us stood motionless after bowing politely to the president's back.

The president sat and wrote for a long time, not paying any attention to us. Beside me stood another example of a practicant's misery, this one was a fairly decent version of a human. I muttered a joke into his ear, I don't know which one anymore, but surely not a good one since he didn't laugh at all. That upset me and I repeated the joke and accompanied it with a tickle. It worked this time, my fellow practicant burst out laughing – everyone was taken aback, each and every one hushed – the president rose.

He got up, and spoke, "I have called you in to let you know that your composition has disgraced our office within all the higher circles. Some of you churn out elephants while others generate mere tadpoles, but I haven't seen a passable sentence – that is one of medium length – from you in a long time, actually at no time. And that results from the fact that you simply ramble on in your writing and cease to think, or else you soon get tired of any brainwork at all, there's no seriousness, no sincerity. And then, it is also clear that you can't even speak German properly, and I can tell you why: because you keep on chattering in Czech! Therefore, I hereby forbid you to speak as much as a word of Czech in the office and I advise you as your friend and superior to do the same outside the office, and to improve your composition by keen reading. Now go back to your work, gentlemen, and keep in mind that no one will be promoted without being accomplished in composition!"

A great hulabaloo got under way all over the office and everyone went around from one clerk to the next to gather up some scraps from the German "kitchen". Whoever could find an old issue of the German magazine *Bohemia* somewhere at home was considered a somebody.

The Czech prattling ceased. Except perhaps when two colleagues knew each other well and were sure the other was not a squealer, then they would exchange a few words in Czech in the hall or in the deathly still archive. They seemed to me similar to secret snuff takers.

I continue to speak Czech loudly; everybody loathes me.

Act one of today's bureaucratic drama is over. The boss makes an exit like Moliere's *le malade imaginaire* does at the end of Act One. Conversation starts to flow during the *entr' acte*.

Discussion at the desk to my right:

"Today is Friday, I can't wait to have my wife's dumplings, she makes them such that they just melt in your mouth."

"You don't eat meat on Fridays?"

"Oh yes, half a pound for everyone as always. Why cook anything else! We observe only major days of fasting and then we treat ourselves to a bit of fish. At least once in a while a bit of fish is good for you!"

"Well, I would fancy a bit of boar with dumplings and an omelet. Children – although you have no children – need to have flour in their meals. Last year my sister-in-law sent us a bunch of snails, so my wife sautéed them."

"Eating wild duck on fasting days, that I can understand, they live on water; but snails creep in gardens, don't they?"

"I was told that snails once lived in water only. They actually creep as if they were swimming, and they're dumb creatures like fish, so there you have it! It's strange that fish don't eat meat, they must know they were meant for fasting!" ...

Discussion at the desk to my left:

"The president is right. These people are foolish, no doubt! All that blabbing they do! We need German and that's that, how else could we write! And if you want to have your children study some French, that's fine, too!"

"It can't hurt!"

"My daughter wouldn't speak Czech on the street under any circumstances. When I sometimes forget myself and speak a word of Czech to her on the street, she starts to blush and tells me: 'But Papa, how can you do this!'"

"Yes, that's right!"

"The other day I read in the paper that they want to create some sort of a universal language. What lunacy!"

"God wouldn't allow that!"

"Everybody should learn German and that's that!"

"True!"

The person closest to the door hushes, "ssh!" Everyone gets quickly back to their desks. The boss enters with his vest undone.

"I feel I'm going to burst gaining weight like this! I have to see either my doctor or a midwife!"

Exercise in laughter.

* * *

Where there is such poverty of mind there is also material poverty. That's how it is! I've been marveling at the shallow and empty lives these people lead.

Perhaps two thirds of them deposit their salaries with a Jew, who rations out to them whatever he pleases on the first of the month.

An old tea-lady that comes to our office gets paid on the first, and on the second they are buying on credit again. I've never heard of anyone inviting someone else over for a visit; maybe they are ashamed of their households.

One can then understand many a thing!

Today I was notified by the president to have my hair, which is rather too long, cut. When hell freezes over!

I have an ally now. The handsomest of clerks took my advice and started signing his name as Wenzl *Narcissus Poeticus* Walter. One such prettified document fell into the hands of the president, who promptly stormed in to bawl him out. He railed at him to completely abandon any such nonsense and work hard instead, and he said he shrinks from the stench of this laziness.

But I know what the president truly shrinks from in connection with the most handsome!

* * *

Having confidence that Mr. Eber wouldn't tell on me, I lied my way into getting time off. I said that my grandmother, whose heir I am, is on her deathbed. The boss did give me time off, but commented sternly that a practicant shouldn't even have a grandmother.

8 At the Funeral

It is noon of the third day, Wednesday, and the house is getting ready to prepare the body of old Žanýnka for burial.

On a black, cloth-covered bier in the shadowy courtyard stands a simple, yet quite well-made casket, lacquered black and decorated with four guilded bear paws. On the lid is a guilded cross, around it lies a myrtle crown with a wide, white ribbon hanging from it. There is about a two-foot high black tetragonal tablet decorating the bier on each longitudinal side, and on it are bulgy silver decorations with figures, the emblem of the funeral society.

With the exception of Mr. Lakmus, who is watching from an upstairs window, and Josefinka's ill sister, who is standing on a footstool and gazing over the railing of the second storey, all the residents of the house we are already familiar with are gathered down in the courtyard, dressed for the occasion. Among them we take notice of a few faces of gentlemen and ladies whom we do not know at all. One does not have to be too quick-witted to tell from their solemn, bleak, habitually strained faces that they are Žanýnka's relatives. A host of women and children from the neighbourhood stand over the courtyard and on the steps.

A priest with a sexton and acolytes has just arrived and begins to pray. Mrs. Bavor and the innkeeper stand beside each other near the door to Žanýnka's apartment. Already the first word of this monotonous recitation have moved Mrs. Bavor to tears and her chin has turned red and is shimmering in genuine sorrow. The innkeeper peers coldly and, showing no consideration for her neighbour's tears, turns to her and starts to converse.

"These people came rushing in like Jews to an auction! They never cared about her while she was alive and now they hasten in for their inheritance! God bless their acquisition, but we wouldn't have stolen anything from them; they didn't need to close everything up and put the bier in the courtyard. Did they give you anything from their endowment for your services? No?"

"Not a scrap!" whispered Mrs. Bavor in a quivering voice. "And they won't!"

"I'm not asking for anything anyway. God bless her, I served her out of Christian love."

The prayers were over, the coffin sprinkled. A black clad "brother" picked up the ornaments, the municipal servants took up the coffin and carried it through the passageway and out onto the street.

There were several fiacres standing behind the hearse. Žanýnka's relatives climbed into the first ones, the landlord and landlady and Miss Matylda, and Josefinka and her mother boarded the remaining ones, and Mrs. Lakmus and Miss Klára got on the last one. Mrs. Lakmus called on the doctor to board with them, and since there was still enough room for one more person in the fiacre, she looked around for anyone still looking for a place.

The innkeeper, Mrs. Bavor and Václav were still standing there together.

"Ladies, one of you can board with us!"

Both women made a move towards the fiacre in the same instant. The innkeeper looked out of the corner of her eye at Mrs. Bavor. They approached the fiacre together and went to put their foot up on the step. This was too much for the innkeeper. She grabbed the handle and turned to Mrs. Bavor sharply, "I am a burgher's wife, aren't I?!" she snarled and climbed onto the fiacre.

Mrs. Bavor was left standing stupefied. Her thoughts froze. Having seen and heard everything, Václav walked up to his mother. "Why don't you and I go on foot, Mother, somebody has to walk!" he said forcefully decisive. "And if we like we can take a coach at the city gate and ride all the way to the cemetery." His mother had not uttered a single word to her son since the landlord's official announcement yesterday. Now she was reluctant to speak, but her struggle lasted only a moment before she agreed, "Of course, we'll walk! Riding doesn't agree with me, anyway. So we won't take a coach. If you'd like to come along, we can take the shortcut on the footpath from the city gate to Košíře. I will walk for the poor deceased woman, I was of help to her many a time while she was alive and have served her since her death. Why wouldn't I take a few steps for her out of Christian love!"

"Then please hang on to me!" said Václav softly, offering her his arm.

"I don't want to be led like some high rank woman – I wouldn't even know how!"

"But this is not for high rank people! I will simply give you support, it's a long way and you're exhausted by your sorrow – do hang on to me, Mother!" He took her arm himself and linked it with his.

The hearse started to move. Walking behind it were only Václav and his mother. Václav walked proudly as if beside a noble duchess. Mrs. Bavor felt so free she could hardly speak. She felt as if she alone had arranged the whole funeral for poor Žanýnka.

9 Further Proof of the Saying

The evening "chat" time was slowly approaching. The daylight was still ivory coloured, yet the colour seemed to be anticipating imminent slumber gradually creeping in. People were almost motionless, it was just the moment when work had already stopped, but the desire for the evening prattle and amusement had not yet come.

The doctor was sitting at his desk. He appeared truly lost in thought. He was pondering over something serious and he evidently wanted to carry out something serious; he pushed the inkwell back and forth, moving pens with fine horn penholders around, examining their flexible points over and over. Now he pulled out a drawer and took out a half-full pad of thin paper. He took a sheet, held it up in

front of him for a moment, opened his mouth wide whereupon a loud "yes" resounded from his full chest, and then he meticulously folded the sheet lengthwise in half

It was obviously a matter of extreme importance as the doctor presently got up and walked through the room as if to take a rest. He walked strangely, staggering about, taking now two steps ahead and now one back, his head either sinking to his chest, or being held up with forced courage.

"Yes," he gasped again. "If it has to happen – and it does – let it come as fast as possible! I'm stranded so I must act with determined haste. Oh, that old Lakmus woman won't let go of me – and neither will Klára – she's a good girl – but I've made up my mind! I can't stay here any longer, everything has to be taken care of within the next few days. Tomorrow I will deliver the third poem to Josefinka in person. I will start a conversation, give her the poem to read and watch my dearest kitten's every tremble, and then we'll settle everything presently. But I'll write the official requisition right away today – I'm in the mood ..."

The doctor wrapped himself in his housecoat and tied the belt as if to protect himself from the cold. He sat down decisively at his desk, dipped his pen into the inkwell, waved it several times above the sheet of paper, then lowered it and a large, black, crafted 'H' appeared on the paper.

Without delay he carried on briskly and accurately, setting one letter down after another. He wrote as follows:

"Honoured Municipal Magistrate of the Royal Capital of Prague!

The undersigned hereby wishes to proclaim his intent to espouse Miss ..."

He peered at it and shook his head. "It's not because of my glasses – it's getting dark, I will close the windows and turn on the light!"

Then he suddenly heard light knocking on his door. He quickly grabbed a blank sheet of paper and placed it upon the letter in progress. Then he forced out a feeble, "Come in."

Václav entered.

"I hope I'm not disturbing you, Doctor," he closed the door behind himself.

"Oh, no – please do come in," grumbled the doctor in a hesitant, suddenly hoarse voice. "I was actually just about to begin something – but do take a seat! What brings you here?"

He asked the question out of habit rather than in reference to the paper scroll Václav was holding in his hand; the foggy bewilderment that obscured his vision prevented him from looking closely at Václav.

Václav sat down. "I have something for you, Doctor, to soothe your nerves in moments of distraction. It's a flimsy novel with no profound message but you may still find it amusing. Simple idea, perhaps even poor, but with an original approach – I detest using the prevailing conventional form and subject for the novel. We'll see what you think of this first attempt ..." and he put the scroll down on the doctor's table. Václav's every movement was youthfully fresh.

"You're always playing with something – well, you're young, after all," the doctor smiled. "And how are you doing, Václav?"

"Not so well now, and it looks like it's going to get even worse! They'll probably kick me out of the office – they found some notes of mine in which I satirized the president. The landlord is in charge of my case."

"Poor, careless young man!" the doctor said, clasping his hands. "And what are you going to do?"

"What am I going to do? Nothing! I will become a writer!"

"Yeah, yeah, yeah!"

"I'd become a writer sooner or later anyhow – and I believe I'm ready now! Or do you mean to say, Doctor, that I'm not talented enough?"

"It takes great talent to be a great writer and small writers won't help our nation. The small ones are mere evidence of our intellectual deficiency, they impoverish the people's spirit, and when there's a need for anything substantial, people look for it abroad. Only an author capable of absolutely original ideas has the right to enter literature. We have more than enough skilled hack-writers!"

"Right you are, Doctor, and since you hold such enlightened views, I absolutely trust your judgement. I agree with you – I take it as a standard for myself. If we leave words like 'great' and 'small' aside, I daresay, perhaps even with some arrogance, that I realize the greatness of the goal, and whoever realizes it and still finds enough courage to pursue it, is justified, and knows at least that much. I won't chain myself to filling up literary gaps, I won't follow a stereotypical pattern. The position of European literature in general will be my position. I will write in a modern way, that is, truthfully, take my characters from real life, describe life in its nakedness, I will say explicitly what I think and feel. How could I not break through like that?"

"Hmm – do you have money?"

"You mean on me? Only about two guilders, but I'm afraid I can't – "

"No – no! I mean, do you have any capital!"

"But you know I don't –"

"Well, then you won't break through. If you had enough capital to live off and still had something left for publishing each of your fine novels, in ten years' time you would gain recognition and your writing could then perhaps appear by a means other than self-publishing. But this way you won't get anywhere. You will have your first such independent writing published on credit and won't be able to sell it, and you won't even get around to a second one. They will pounce on you first of all because of your independence, which is not tolerated in small families and small nations, and second of all because, while depicting the truth, you knocked the small world and the small people. The more spiteful will say you are talentless, or perhaps even idiotic, the kinder will say you are crazy. It won't be much publicity for you ..."

"Who wants publicity?"

"One needs a bit of it in the beginning, our people believe in printed matter, they don't care about anything that hasn't been validated for them. At the same time, however, the publicity given to others will impair you. They will become greater, while you remain stuck, become resentful, perhaps engage in literary foolishness, perhaps become weary of writing altogether. On top of that your financial situation will remain dire. There won't be any other way than to take up hack writing. That will bring about a dislike for writing. You will limit it to the bare minimum, become bitter or lazy, and you'll be finished, starting all over will be impossible!"

"Well, it surely won't be exactly like that! I'm expecting to succeed from the very start. Have you already read the volume of my poems that I gave you?"

"I have."

"Well then, what do you say?"

"In short, it reads well – some of the verses are nice – but what are verses good for? You'd be better off burning them!"

Václav jumped out of his seat; the doctor also got up spontaneously and leaned with his hand on the table. For a moment there was silence. Václav stepped to the window and pressed his forehead against it. But he soon spoke again in an uneasy voice.

"You're going to the wedding on Sunday, Doctor?"

"The wedding? – What wedding?"

"Josefinka told me that you will be the witness! I will be the best man."

"And who is getting married?"

"You didn't know that Josefinka is marrying chief machinist Bavorák this Sunday?"

Everything turned black before the doctor's eyes, his head was spinning, he sank heavily into the chair.

Václav leapt towards the slumped man and bent over him.

"Are you all right – is anything the matter?"

He got no response – only a repeated rattle told him that help was needed. He dashed to the door and cried, "Mrs. Lakmus – Miss Klára – bring water and a light quick – the doctor isn't feeling well!" Then he approached the reclining doctor and began to take off his tie and loosen his housecoat.

Mrs. Lakmus came running in with a lighted lamp followed by Miss Klára.

"Water – get water here quick!" ordered Václav.

Meanwhile, the doctor opened his eyes. He heard Václav's words. "No – no – no water!" he uttered painstakingly. "I'm feeling fine now! It's just from the heat today – it happens to me sometimes in summer!"

"Go!" ordered Mrs. Lakmus, "and get water with a bit of raspberry syrup – we have all that at home – go, Klára!"

Miss Klára left in haste.

"You're fine, now," said Václav, "But you really had me scared! And it was actually not so hot today! But everything's fine now and you're in good hands, so I'll take my leave! Good-bye, Doctor, good-bye, Madam!"

"Good-bye," replied the doctor with a forced smile, "and what I said to you was meant well!"

"I have no doubt about that, and thank you. Good-bye!" Václav departed.

Miss Klára brought syrup on a tray. The doctor put up some resistance but in the end he did help himself to the cooling drink.

"Drink up now, dear son-in-law," urged Mrs. Lakmus. "We'll stay with you for an hour or so. I was planning a surprise visit with Klára for today anyhow. The two of you are like children, timid and shy. If it wasn't for me you would never have gotten anywhere. Oh, dear – In my fright I put the lamp right on the doctor's white sheet of paper, I didn't even see where I was putting it!"

She lifted the lamp and the papers shifted aside. As the top sheet slipped away, Mrs. Lakmus couldn't help peering at the letter. The doctor was speechless, shocked once again.

Mrs. Lakmus' face cheered up like a sunny sky. "That's marvelous, marvelous indeed!" she said. "Look, Klára, the doctor is already composing an application for a marriage license! Look, he's already about to write your name! But you must give Klára the pleasure of watching you fill in her name! Please, here's the pen!" The doctor sat frozen in his chair.

"Come, come, don't be shy!" Mrs. Lakmus dipped the pen and placed it in the doctor's hand. "Klára, come and watch!"

The doctor was suddenly struck by a flash of determination. He gripped the pen, noisily pulled up the chair and added: "Klára Lakmus."

Mrs. Lakmus clasped her hands in excitement. "And now you can give each other a kiss! – Now it's absolutely acceptable! – Don't be shy, you silly goose!"

10 In a Moment of Excitement

The moon stands above Petřín Hill, bright and glittering. The wooded hillside at the top is flooded in misty light and offers a dreamy, poetic view, as if through clear waters at an underwater forest. Many an eye wanders or casts anchor somewhere on the hillside, each apparently absorbed in deep thought or a moment of emotional excitement.

Josefinka, leaning out of the second floor window of the rear part of the building, is looking up at the illuminated Petřín; her fiancé is standing beside her. The bright moonlight easily allows us to distinguish the contours of the handsome young man; his round face is rimmed by a bushy fair beard, his eyes radiate with vitality. Josefinka is staring fixedly and quietly in the flood of light while her fiancé frequently turns to look at his girl, whose tiny body he had wrapped his right arm around, and each time he looks at her, he squeezes her gently, ever so gently as if afraid to dust the bloom of the beautiful moment.

Now he leaned over and touched his fiancée's locks with his lips. Josefinka turned to him, took his hand and pressed it against her lips. Then she reached out and touched the fine, thick bunch of myrtle on the window-sill.

"How old would your little sister be now?" she asked in a sombre voice.

"She would now be in full bloom, like you."

"Your mother doesn't know how happy she made me by sending me myrtle for our wedding, and from so far away!"

"Oh she does! Where I'm from everybody believes that myrtle taken from the hands of the dead, planted and preserved until a wedding, is sure to bring good luck. Since the day I took the myrtle from the hands of my little sister lying in her coffin, and planted it in the earth, Mother surely must have prayed over it and watered it with her tears every single day. Mother is infinitely good."

"Same as you," sighed Josefinka and snuggled even closer to her fiancé.

They both fell silent again and looked up into the clear sky as if into a dream about their future.

"You're unusually quiet today," she whispered again at last.

"Real feeling has no tongue, I feel gratified, so gratified that I won't ever be able to find words to describe my present gratification. Don't you feel the same way?"

"I don't even know how I feel. I seem to be different, more exalted. If this feeling should not last, then I'd want to die with it now."

"And the doctor would cry his ditties over your grave," her fiancé teased her. "See," he added in a voice once again serious, "however you look at it, I think that someone who truly loves couldn't even write something like that. I certainly never could – but I think the doctor is playing games with you."

"No, he's a good man."

"Look at her defending him! Say what you will, you're still pleased by those ditties!"

"Well –"

"Aha, I knew it! You women are all the same. You just have to have your sweets, your various heaps of frivolous delicacies. How did I deserve this, I'd like to know."

"Karel!" said Josefinka alarmed, and looked horrified into his eyes unable to recognize him.

"It's true, though!" continued the indignant young man. "If you hadn't been double-dealing with him and me, he wouldn't have had the courage." He gave Josefinka a little shove.

His right arm, which had been wrapped around her slipped back down to his side, only his left hand remained in her hands. Their hands hung together lifelessly.

They both looked up at the sky without uttering a word. It lasted for a long time as they silently, hardly even breathing, stared into space. Suddenly Karel could feel a burning tear fall from Josefinka's eyes onto his hand. He started and cuddled his sobbing sweetheart tightly to himself.

"Forgive me – Josefinka – forgive me!" he pleaded.

The young woman sobbed.

"Please, don't cry! You can be upset with me but don't cry! Hush – I made a mistake, I do know that you could never deceive, that you love me as dearly as I love you!"

"But surely you didn't love me in the moment you pushed me away from you!"

"You're right – it was a wicked moment! I didn't even know I was capable of such silly jealousy! – It was strange, I felt as if I had suddenly suppressed love! – I forgot that

you're young and beautiful, I was a fool, I do know that any young girl that has a healthy body, and is not crippled or too ugly ..."

Suddenly something rustled behind the lovers and they both swiftly turned around.

Josefinka's ill sister Katuška had been sitting in the room behind them all this time. She had sat without moving during the whole scene and the lovers had completely forgotten about the poor soul. During Karel's last words she suddenly rose, took a few steps and, crying bitterly, sank down into a nearby chair.

"Katuška – good God, dear Katuška!" lamented Josefinka.

Both lovers stood with trembling hearts beside the ill, crying Katuška. Their eyes filled with tears, their lips trembled but dared not to utter even words of comfort.

11 A Debut Novel which Begs for Kind Clemency

Doctor Josef Loukota felt rather strange as he awoke to the kiss of the most radiant sun in the world. His head was spinning, he felt as if his brain would burst, his nerves were shivering feverishly. Odd figures were mingling in his imagination: Josefinka, Bavorák, Klára, Mrs. Lakmus and Václav were flashing back and forth; other people, strangers, were also among them, and animals, and so forth.

Suddenly the first coherent and clear thought came to him: he remembered he was engaged to be married. He shuddered; then he sat up in bed. At the same time his gaze fell upon the night table where some papers covered in writing were spread about – and now it finally dawned on the doctor entirely, he realized that yesterday in his excitement he had turned to the flimsy novel brought to him by Václav.

I do not intend to provide a detailed description of the doctor's nervous excitement, my readers are ingenious enough to easily infer the rest, considering the doctor's character and the events which have taken place thus far. But in order to be a little helpful, I feel obliged to report on the doctor's reading material, then the reader has all the clues at hand and is able perhaps even to guess at the doctor's colourful dream.

Here is the novel!

On Some Domestic Animals
A Semi-Bureaucratic Idyll by Václav Bavor

Page seventeen of the diary
of Mr. Ondřej Dílec

...will pay the foreman less, that's for sure, how much does plaster cost, anyway, he can't be paying his bricklayers that much; if I had known, I wouldn't have gone ahead with it so now I'm calling it off. I know that, after all, but since she has nothing but the tavern and a child, and that doesn't bring in much, I could do lots of developing, but her boy and mine make two children already, and who knows how many more may come, and when marrying a widow one has to think about the future. My house is big enough, in any event, and who knows what the future holds, but I won't do anything now and I didn't sleep a wink last night, and anyway, she's put me off by now. She wants to force my hand with that milksop, but that won't work, a settled down woman like her should know better than that, it doesn't matter if he has an education, what will become of him, a doctor, a professor or an editor, so what? Too bad she has a six-month notice agreement, otherwise she'd be moving out this instant, and he's not going to marry her, which she knows very well, but she just wants to make trouble. But you just wait, I'll turn the tables on you, and when the landlord has to he can always find a way, and I already know what I'm going to do today. Then you can go calling "chick, chick, chick, chick" when I'm crossing the courtyard as if you didn't see me, so that you wouldn't have to greet me and stutter out "good morning," today...

Private Letter from Jan Střepeníčko,
Practicant at the Municipal Council, to Josef Pískčík,
Junior Clerk at the Same Office

Dear Friend and Honoured Patron!

I am certain you will forgive my turning to Your Eminence with this plea. You kindly promised to support me with your influence as well as your exceptional experience during my clerical career. Forgive me, however, for not seeking you in person with my matter; you know yourself that the Magistrate councillors do not look keenly upon a practicant popping into a different bureau rather than remaining sitting at his own desk.

But now let me get straight to the point and to my request so that I don't take up too much of your time! The head secretary ordered me to file all documents that have arrived by yesterday according to the cases to which they pertain. He considers it, I believe, a kind of a test, and due to my inexperience I feel at quite a loss about one of the records. Allow me to acquaint Your Excellency with the puzzling document.

A Prague landlord, Mr. Ondřej Dílec of building registration number 1213-I accuses Mrs. Helenka Velebová of keeping, for her own unnecessary amusement, an excessive number of hens, capons and roosters, whereas the latter crow unreasonably early in the morning and in doing so break the slumber of the tenants in the above-mentioned building. The complainant therefore asks that the accused be prohibited from keeping poultry.

So this is the content of the document that I do not know where to file. I would have sent the document to Your Eminence for personal inspection, but as you are well aware, I cannot take a chance by borrowing an official document. I beg you for your benevolent and, according to your judgement, perhaps even brief advice, and hope you will not take offence if I ask you to send your response sealed.

Your most loyal
Jan Střepeníčko

Official Notification N.C. 13211 to Mr. Edvard Jungmann, Doctor of Medicine.

The Municipal Council hereby notifies you as a committee member that you are to report to Room 35 at City Hall on August 4th, thence to proceed with an official assigned to you to building registration number 1213-I to inspect a matter that falls under the jurisdiction of the Ministry of Health.

City Council Official
Prague, August 2nd, 1858.

Private Letter from Mrs. Helenka Velebová, Innkeeper,
to her sister Alojsie Trousilová, married teacher in Chrudim

Dear Sister,

Many greetings and kisses from me and little Toníček, who asks you to send him something. Ask your husband if he still remembers the Kalhotkas' Jan, the youngest one, he is grown up by now and schooled, and he wants to be a teacher, too. He may still remember him because he used to come home for the holidays, I had forgotten all about him and you wouldn't recognize him either, he's grown so big and strong. He used to take meals with me for two months and only then we negotiated an arrangement as he had no money, as is often the case with students, especially those who are worth anything, but he's not a rogue, besides he's already finished his studies and he's sending you and your husband his best regards. Kalhotka is a very cheerful fellow and his sincerety always makes me laugh. He published poems he wrote about me, you know the foolish kind of stuff, though as a teacher I'm sure you know about things like that, he wrote there I was like a "starry night" and such nonsense that I thought I was going to die laughing, but it did look neat all printed in the magazine, and above it all was written in bold letters TO HER, which meant me.

To your husband you can say it's none of his business whether I get married again or not, so he should quit teasing me. It's true, though, that I am too young to live singly and my child needs a father and there are enough men to choose from. Our landlord Dílec would also like to get me but he's a clumsy man and also wants lots of money which I don't have as I barely manage to make ends meet. Dílec isn't very bright and he's jealous of Kalhotka, so he filed a complaint with the Magistrate that I rear too many hens and roosters that bother the tenants, especially with their crowing early in the morning. I had a good laugh when a couple of gentlemen came here wanting to see those flocks of roosters but I didn't have any, since I only keep enough poultry for my own use and for guests. The landlord will be fuming, but it serves him right, I don't know why he's like that when I'm not interested in him. Besides, he's also not exactly a blooming youth anymore.

I'm sending along the hat for Fanynka, I had cherries put on it instead of roses so I hope it won't be too oud, and please be so kind as to let me know for how much you could get me clarified butter, it would perhaps still cost me less than in Prague. Sorry about talking so much here, but who should I talk to if I don't have anyone and I'm of good cheer by nature.

Your faithful sister,
Helenka.
P. S. Got to go.

Page Four of the Record Taken at the Senate Session,
15 of August, 1858.

...endorsed the schedule recommended by Councillor Veřej, as only matters of importance have their place before the Senate. Thereupon the Senate proceeded to item number seven. Councillor Veřej reported on the complaint of Mr. Ondřej Dílec, owner of building registration number 1213-I, against Mrs. Helenka Velebová, innkeeper at the same place. Mr. Ondřej Dílec complains that the innkeeper, Velebová, holds an excessive amount of poultry that bother the other tenants with their morning crowing. The councillor read the report of a commission completed by Messrs. Edvard Jungman, doctor of medicine, and Josef Píščík, junior clerk. It is evident from the report that the commission has carefully examined the matter at the location in question and found the defendant had no more than two hens in the courtyard, one rooster and one capon exclusively for the occasion that any of her guests should have a fancy for poultry.

The presiding magistrate puts forth that there are no measures to be taken, particularly due to the fact that the amount of poultry in question is so low and it is not possible to order the innkeeper to store them all slaughtered.

Councillor Veřej points out that the complainant, Mr. Dílec, is also somewhat hard of hearing, and therefore the problem with crowing is not likely to inconvenience him greatly. The councillor hence proposes the complaint be dropped.

The proposition was passed by a vote of one. Thereupon the Senate proceeded to item number ...

*Private Letter from Mrs. Helenka Velebová, innkeeper, to her
sister Alojsie Trousilová, married teacher in Chrudim.*

Sister!

Greetings and many kisses from me as well as little Toníček, although I'm truly upset with you for acting so old
even though you're actually younger; even if you are a teacher, what of it, it's not going to make you any wiser than
me, so don't put on airs, we know how things go, and who
knows what you'd do if you were a widow. I do not want Dílec, no way, and I won't let anyone force him on me. You
wouldn't want anyone that has caused you injury either. It's
none of his business whether I'm fat or skinny, so what if he
says he could make three cadets out of me, who asked for his
opinion anyway? If he doesn't like my appearance, why
doesn't he stop running after me, I don't want him, I tell
you. And did he have to file complainy against me if he has
such affection for me? He lost the case anyway, and now he
can't even stand to look at me. But I'll settle accounts with
him, everything is already set up. A certain gentleman, not
Kalhotka this time, don't worry, I'm not a fickle spring chick-
en to be going after students, although it would be nobody's
business, I'm my own woman and won't be ordered around,
(besides Kalhotka is better than you think), anyhow, he
remembered that the law prohibits the breeding of pigs in
the city of Prague and Dílec has two pigs in the garden,
running around all day long. Little Toníček always plays
with them, but that's beside the point, we've already filed
a complaint, Dílec will be infuriated, and it serves him
right. You take offence at everything, and it is unfortunate
that you find your hat too loud, maybe you can tell it to shut
up! Pardon me, but you know how I am, always saying what
I think, besides we're sisters, so it goes without saying. Your
faithful sister,

Helenka
P. S. Got to go.

*Confidential Letter Written by His Worship of the Royal
Capital of Prague, Addressed to Mr. Veřej, City Councillor*

Dear Councillor!

As I will not be able to meet with you in person anymore
today to discuss a certain matter with you, and will be staying

at my villa tomorrow, I am writing you this letter. The matter in question concerns the complaint of Mrs. Helena Votrubová against Ondřej Dílec, owner of building registration number 1213-I, against whom she has launched a complaint for the illegal keeping of pigs. The complaint has now come *ad manus inclitissimi praesidii* for the second time from Solicitor Zajíček, who, as you are aware, is one of the opponents of the current city council. As I have been informed, this matter has already been dealt with once before, thoughnot in a thorough manner. The municipal executive and the district Medical Officer have examined the case and determined that as Mr. Dílec keeps merely a pair of piglets which he breeds for his own consumption, no further measures would be taken. It was not suitable of you, dear Council Official, to deal with such an important matter *brevi manu*, on your own in the absence of the senate. It is beyond any doubt that piglets classify as pigs, and breeding pigs is, of course, strictly prohibited in the City of Prague. In addition, since at this time, in the fall, the *cholera morbus* commonly occurs we may suffer serious consequences with this matter, since Solicitor Zajíček undoubtedly will proceed with his case. Therefore, considering the immediate and hazardous nature of the case, I urge you, dear Councillor, to order a new inspection and examination of the case immediately, followed without delay by a Senate debate in my presence, that would conclude the proceeding so as to order the *ex senatu concluso* removal of the objectionable herd within eight days.

Prague, on this the, 17th day of September, 1858.

Private Letter from Jan Kalhotka, Teaching Aspirant, to his Friend Emil Blažíček, substitute teacher in Písek.

In *nomine domini* I bring you happy tidings that I have been appointed the position of substitute teacher in Hradec Králové, a fortress, a town, and a place with a gymnasium. Well now, off I go to tackle the Czech future and like you labour on the "inherent role of a nation," which quotation you may already have read somewhere. I am looking forward to my noble vocation and new career with all my heart, especially since, as I hear, there are a great number of pretty girls in Hradec Králové and I quite fancy that. I'm quite lucky with women, I don't think I'd need to do anything with the exception of love and everything else would take care of itself and I'd have a grand time. I have lately been strapped for money, which occasionally somehow happens to me, and yet I've been living like a baron, or rather a happy innkeeper. Imagine, a young widow with an inn, on top of that she's from my hometown, and I'm a fellow in the prime of his life – well, I've been living cheaply, very cheaply. But my widow isn't doing so well, her landlord wanted to marry her but she refused because she loves me, now he's given her notice and she's at her wits' end. I do have a heart and because I've managed to get a little bit of money together, I'm not going to her anymore so I wouldn't stand in the way of her happiness. Women are smart, especially widows, I'm sure she'll work it out. After all, I can't say she and the landlord wouldn't be a good match, they'd make a nice couple, I can just see them in harmony eating kidney and salad on Sundays. You can tell that I wasn't playing a game with her, nor was I unconcerned about her, otherwise I wouldn't have written so much about her. But – what to do with her – that's the thing!

I'm ending my letter with a wholehearted wish that you may also have a grand time.

Yours –

Vice-regent's Ordinance Delivered to Mr. Ondřej Dílec, Owner of Building Registration Number 1213–I, Regarding his Appeal against the Municipal Council's Decision.

...the stated objections cannot be considered of significance as keeping pigs is forbidden by law in the City of Prague and the fact that His Worship keeps a pair of horses, which cause even more manure and problems, is absolutely irrelevant to this case. Mr. Ondřej Dílec is, therefore, hereby fined five Austrian guilders and ordered to have his pigs either slaughtered, or removed from the City of Prague in another way, otherwise official measures such as elimination or translocation will be taken should he fail to comply within three days.

Delivered in Prague, on this, the 14th day of October, 1858.

Private Letter from Mrs. Helenka Velebová, innkeeper, to her
sister Alojsie Trousilová, a married teacher in Chrudim.

Dear Sister!

You're right, see, I admit it, and it's all because you're wise and learned from your husband while I'm a witless fool the same way my late husband was. But don't chide me about Kalhotka anymore, it's all over, he's run away; you know that their whole family was like that and Mother never liked them, but it's not my fault, he would talk and talk, and you know how we women are, and that I have a kind heart. You're right also about Dílec, it's all up to me, if I only knew how to go ahead with it. He really dried up! You can see he's troubled by it, but he's stubborn and he thinks he's something special since he's a landlord, even though it's true he has no debts and he's out and out a good man. The other day I was playing with his little boy – what a sweet child, he's got such big blue eyes and adorable cheeks, and he's only half a year younger than my little Toníček – and they were playing together again and little Toníček goes up to their place, and one time Dílec was on his way home but I pretended not to see him and kissed the boy, and he stood there waiting but didn't say a word, and then went on but didn't send for his son as he usually does. Thank you for the butter, it wasn't very cheap and I could have gotten it at the market in Prague for the same price, but the quality is good. We still have five weeks to go before St. Catherine's Day and tomorrow I'll bring the rent to Dílec myself, but I tell you I'll

feel so ashamed, but you see it's nice of him that he's not even pressing me for it. Little Toníček sends many kisses and asks you to send him something nice. Kisses and greetings from me to you and your husband.

Your always faithful sister,
Helenka.
P. S. Got to go.

The diary of Mr. Ondřej Dílec, page thirty-one

...never had such wonderful Christmas holidays. Helenka is a good housekeeper and a good cook and loves me dearly, and she's not as bad as I had thought, she obeys me to the letter and she's almost better than my poor first wife – may she rest peace – now I do believe that she didn't really love that student youth, women are so strange when they want to tease the person they are truly in love with. If she stays the way she is now, and she will, I can tell already, she will have no regrets, she'll see that I'll make a good father for her child and that I haven't forgotten about him and have provided for them even if I should die today or tomorrow, I will also have the building whitewashed in the spring and we'll make the garden into a restaurant with a band, things are much better already, nothing goes right when you have bare hands. And now hopefully I will be left in peace with all these lawsuits, today two gentlemen came regarding my appeal to Vienna, but I had forgotten all about it and I was staring at them for a long time not knowing what the matter was, an order came from Vienna to carefully re-examine the whole case, but how can it be re-examined when I finished the last pork sausage today for breakfast? Helenka was howling with laughter and she has lots of grease in the kitchen, but now I don't know who would have won and ...

12 Five Minutes After the Recital

A thin childlike soprano faded away in an astonishingly high pitch, Miss Valinka closed her sheet of music, the accompanying musician struck a few more final chords, and a well-learned smile with a suitable bow signaled the end of the recital.

"Bravo – she'll be a real artist – wow, and you'll be a happy man, Mr. Eber!" exulted Mrs. Bauer, stopped clapping and got up from her seat so that she could embrace Valinka in genuine, heartfelt excitement. The people behind her got up – there were about twenty of them gathered here in two rows in the parlour – and showered Valinka with kisses such that the admired girl had hardly even a chance to catch her breath and cry out, "But – my hair – mum!"

Mr. Eber, who had been standing between a pillar and a window throughout the whole recital, swallowed, blinked back the emotion, then uttered in a shaky voice, "Well, we'll have her take lessons for about two more years, and then they can have her. She'll be only fourteen then and people will be surprised, but what of it, talent will be the decisive factor. Would you believe, Mrs. Bauer, that she made such progress in her twenty lessons of French that she could easily communicate with her teacher?"

Mrs. Bauer clasped her hands in amazement. "Is that so! Valinka, is it true?"

"O oui, madame!" Valinka confirmed.

"See, I was surprised myself. But it's also because she has good teachers. Her singing teacher is especially good. He has a really good method paying attention to every detail, he even puts his thumb in her mouth if she doesn't open it right. But I will not keep her in Prague!"

"Of course not, that would be a sin," agreed Mrs. Bauer and sat back down beside her daughter. Miss Marie, who had been sitting to the right side of her friend's beau, Lieutenant

Kořínek, deliberately removed both her gloves after the recital for a vigorous applause. Lieutenant Kořínek, a man of weak stature and sickly appearance with a permanent, yet apparently frozen, smile on his toothless mouth, applauded along with her.

"I'm beginning to feel quite hot," said the young lady, her duty done, to her neighbour, who was still toiling. "We girls don't have any strength. The child sings beautifully, doesn't she?"

"She certainly does!" agreed the lieutenant. "Particularly that C at the end was quite excellent."

"But that was perhaps only an F?" pointed out the young lady.

"Oh, no, it was a C and before that one there was another C; when it's so high, it's always a C."

Miss Marie's face grew long and froze. "So you are musical, too?" she asked, if only to say something.

"Me? No, I was told I didn't have any talent. But my brother used to play even from sheet music, and he would play each piece with great precision the first and any other time."

"I used to have a brother like that myself," sighed the young lady. "He passed away, poor soul. A beautiful tenor! From high C, as you first mentioned, all the way down to A, I tell you all the way to A!"

"That must have been splendid!"

"Are you a keen music lover?"

"But of course!"

"So you probably go to the opera often?"

"Me? – No! It costs too much money and I have only two ears. Once I did go to see an opera and liked that one – what was it called – darn it – I did like that one. Other times I don't find opera very enjoyable, I'm too much of a soldier and I get upset when I see a big strong fellow that could be beating a Turkish drum actually playing a tiny little violin. I also don't find it enjoyable when the singer starts her circumflexes or whatever it's called."

Just then Miss Marie turned her head towards her mother who whispered, "So how is the conversation going?"

"Oh fine – I don't think he could tell a match if you showed it to him upside down!"

"That's all right."

"Of course it is," concluded Marie with a whisper, turning

back to her neighbour. "But it's quite nice indeed that they have their child take lessons like that. Especially considering that they themselves don't have anything at all. They're up to their eyes in debt, we have investments in this house and I always tell Mother to be careful but she's so goodhearted."

The news evidently gave Mr. Kořínek a start, he began to say something, ask a few questions, but just at that moment general commotion indicated that the guests were ready to depart. Miss Marie and Mrs. Bauer got up, too.

"We have such a long way to go to get home and we're walking alone," complained Miss Marie to the lieutenant. "I've never had any gentlemen friends and truly chivalrous men are so hard to find!"

"Perhaps if you would allow me ..." the lieutenant readily began with a gallant smile.

"Oh, that would be wonderful – Mommy, Mr. Kořínek said he would walk us home!"

"It's a long way! But Mr. Kořínek can stay with us for dinner, it's true, and we'll have a time of it!"

The landlady was bidding good-bye to the guests one by one, Miss Matylda, who had to leave Mr. Kořínek for a moment in order to socialize politely with her guests, was just distributing kisses when Mrs. Eber whispered something into her ear. Miss Matylda then approached the lieutenant and whispered, "You'll stay, won't you, Mother would like to invite you for a bit of ham."

"I – I'm –"

"Ah, my dear Matylda," Miss Marie stepped up to her and began to embrace her friend warmly, "you've treated us to such a performance! It's only a shame it didn't last longer, normally I'm afraid to walk home alone, but Mr. Kořínek has just offered his company since we live so far away from here! Well then, adieu, angel, just one more kiss, there! Your humble servant, madam!"

Miss Matylda paled and stood there petrified.

"Well, why don't you see Miss Marie to the door," urged the landlady, "What's with you? – Oh –," she gasped involuntarily, seeing the lieutenant preparing to depart with the Bauers.

"Adieu, angel," nodded Miss Marie and drifted to the door. Miss Matylda stood frozen to the spot.

13 After the Draw

Mrs. Bavor was quite comfortably seated behind the counter since on Friday afternoons, until a few evening customers arrived, there was nothing to do even in a grocer's shop. Her husband was somewhere in town attending to business matters, Václav hardly ever spent any time at home anyway, and Mrs. Bavor was sitting here all alone entertaining herself with her dream-books spread out in front of her, sheets of paper covered with numbers and other things. She was enjoying herself, though, and even if she yawned a little here and there, she did so in evident contentment, her cheeks were radiant, and her eyes were glowing softly from behind her spectacles.

Just then, she glanced toward the door as someone had just entered. It was the innkeeper. Mrs. Bavor pretended not to notice her arrival and went on busying herself with her numbers. There can be no doubt that the event at the funeral of the late Žanýnka is still casting its gloomy shadow over this day. The innkeeper advanced on into the room. "Praised be the name of the Lord," she greeted.

"Now and for ever more," answered Mrs. Bavor without even lifting her head.

"So, did we win anything?" the innkeeper said by way of starting a conversation.

"Well, there's not much that we won together," retorted Mrs. Bavor coldly, emphasizing her last word.

"Together – hmm – so it's true then, a customer told me that you had entered the line again, the way you had it before and you hit the jackpot." Every word was sharp, inquisitive.

"Yes – when I listen to my own old head, I always make the right decision."

"And do I get a share of the jackpot?"

"Well, I don't see any reason why you should!"

"What a sham!"

Mrs. Bavor's face turned white as a sheet. Yet she still didn't raise her head and went on to answer slowly and in a cold voice. "Have you contributed any money towards my line? Your advice was to change the numbers, and you put your money on the changed numbers and you won a double, half of it is yours. And that's that."

Mrs. Bavor's coldness, even if forced, nevertheless made an impact on the innkeeper. "But there's no need to quarrel about that," she said with equally forced meekness, "I wish to everyone what God bestows upon them, so why wouldn't I wish this for you, your Václav and my Márinka – they do love each other so."

"There's no hurry – they're young, so why force it – besides, I have low tolerance for haughtiness, my son is a grocer's son, and he will become what may. So there!"

"Well, I hope you don't think I have to kowtow to you? There's no need to, my daughter is once and for all a burgher's daughter and no one can take that away from her!"

"She can have it for dinner," replied Mrs. Bavor spitefully, taking off her spectacles.

"Honour is honour, you either have it or you don't," hissed the innkeeper, "I can go wherever I please and I'll be admitted everywhere, but you can't make a lumberjack into a gentleman – even if you gild him. That's how I see it, and not another word about it – so long!" and the innkeeper dashed out.

"Your humble servant," Mrs. Bavor cried her farewell and only now raised her head.

She looked outside for a while. Her cheeks were regaining their former colour, her eyes were starting to glow again. "You won't get the better of me!" she said in a loud voice, apparently satisfied that she did not allow her emotions to get carried away.

Mrs. Bavor put on her spectacles once again and started to look through her dream-books and numbers. Since she was a lottery player body and soul, a player of the most distinguished variety whose techniques bordered on science, she was enjoying the highest reputation in this field all over the neighbourhood. A perfect lottery player's work, however, is never quite finished if she wants to keep honing her skills and for this she must make use of every free moment.

Nobody would believe how much preparation needs to be done before one can enter a sure bet in a lottery just once! The right number can be neither calculated with rational coldness nor does it reveal itself in a flash, it may only come as a great coincidence ignored by any level-headed person; the right number is neither a mathematical quantity nor any incorporeal phantom, it comes neither from the intellect nor from the imagination and I could compare it to a flower or, better, a crystal that needs time to begin to flourish and to grow, that requires solid ground, and for a lottery number that solid ground is a person's *heart*. Yes, the heart is the homeland of the number and as the heart is connected with all the rest of the world, as even the farthest star's magnetic field affects the heart, the same way is the number connected to the rest of the world. And due to its origin the number is thus the indisputable property of the female sex, and any time a man butts in, he soon strays and gets bogged down and even drowned in the mud of rational reasoning.

Of all this – though she could not put it into words so eloquently as we – Mrs. Bavor was fully aware. She cultivated her numbers the way a gardener cultivats flowers from the seed, she was as well far removed from the chance "tear-off" games hanging in shops or from tangled up calculations, and the basis for her extensive operations was her dreambook, the *kumbrlík*.

It is doubtlessly a name with a mystical ring to it, if only due to tradition, which is underlined in the distinctive work's full title, which reads: *Interpretations of the Impressions of Dreams of Various Natures Based Upon the Explications of the Divers Origines of Different Categories of Dreams, Including Numbers to Stake in Lotteries in Accordance With the Meanings of Said Dreams.*

The introduction quotes some old sages, it talks about Aristotle and Hector's wife, about the Severi and Virgil's mother, Jacob's ladder and the Pharaoh's cows, about the dream of the Three Magi in the East and Nebuchadnezzar in Babylon, and all this in a style that cannot be comprehended merely by the intellect, but must be understood by feeling.

The correct interpretation of dreams is the basis for lottery playing and an indispensable aid for interpretation is the *kumbrlík*. But not every dream is fit to be interpreted. There are certainly months with very few truly lucky days, these are well known to every experienced practitioner, as these are "beliefs held by ancient astronomers and confirmed by the most supreme ruler of all planets." But a lucky day does not yield a pearl right away either, and only an inexperienced person does not know that there are eight different categories of dreams and only the fifth is the right one. First, it is suitable to omit from interpretation those dreams that arose from an evil spirit (the eighth category), also those that are personal revelations to God-pleasing people (the seventh category). The kinds of dreams that come from an ailment, from being hot-blooded or hot-headed, from water in the liver or in the lungs, are also of no significance. However, the fifth category comes to those who "eat little or nothing at night and simultaneously are of healthy and sound mind." A proper lottery player thus must establish a particular lifestyle for the sake of breeding dreams, and Mrs. Bavor had done so. A suitable dream can then be explained in accordance with the numerical interpretation as stated in the *kumbrlík* (although there are a host of other kinds of dream-books, including illustrated ones, and even though each is helpful in some way, the *kumbrlík* towers over the other dream-books like Sněžka Mountain over Krkonoše) Numbers chosen in this way are not entirely beyond any doubt, but they are entered in the next draw, just to test the waters. If they win right away, fine, if they don't, that's all right too; the lottery receipts will, however, be kept, and not discarded. For lottery players have four different periods for dreams, three hours each; the first one is the seventh hour in the evening, which indicates ancient roots. When the dream will actually come through (whether in eight days or by the third draw, in three months, three years, or – yes – even in twelve years) can be determined for certain according to the period in which the dream came. It is therefore very important for the lottery player to keep her carefully maintained collection of old lottery receipts.

But that by no means exhausts the list of the lottery player's tools. Even though Mrs. Bavor was not concerned with such nonsense as, for instance, putting ninety cut up numbers into a glass with a big garden spider so that it would drag them into its web – she was too sensible for that – she did have a long, linen bag with ninety small balls in it and every day she drew out three with her right hand and three with her left. She carefully recorded the numbers thus obtained, noting the date on special sheets of paper and adding "me", since every day she also had her husband, son, as well as other people she liked draw, and she made a note of all collected numbers, adding the person's name beside the line. Numbers from *public* draws she recorded on a separate sheet of paper, as such a list also has its value, though it is not possible to articulate a law governing the way drawn numbers are repeated, but if you have been keeping an eye on the drawn numbers for a time, all of a sudden you will feel a flinch when looking at a certain line, and that is a hint.

And finally, when the time arrives that a good dream from a good day should be fulfilled, when the same numbers are drawn by both the right and the left hand, and, in addition, the hint comes, well then go and place a bet since there is no doubt of a sure win. Following all this, Mrs. Bavor entered her own, unchanged line with full confidence and hit the jackpot.

I have said that a perfect lottery player's work is never quite finished if she wants to keep honing her skills, and for this she must use every free moment. One jackpot was not going to divert Mrs. Bavor from her cycle, she needed the lottery to sharpen her wit, to please her heart, and for that reason we find her again absorbed in her work.

She was making notes and rewriting and tidying things up when suddenly Václav stepped in. He greeted her and stood before the counter. Mrs. Bavor nodded but continued to work undisturbed. After a while she took the cloth bag with the larger balls, stirred and shook it and then held it out to Václav.

"You haven't drawn yet today – right hand first! I wonder if you already know that today you've been let go from the office," she said in an absolutely calm voice.

"What –," stammered Václav and glanced sharply at his mother, whose calm voice puzzled him.

"One of those you drew is the same as mine, how strange, I keep drawing thirteen! – Yes, the landlord was here and he asked me to tell you. And what's this thing about the hairdresser yesterday? That silly landlords' girl was here at noon saying she was obliged to give you many thanks for doing her a great favour."

"Ah, that was nothing! The landlords had a private recital yesterday and the hairdresser that came to do the miss' hair fell behind the mangle and couldn't get out. I rushed there and pulled him out, Márinka happened to be there…"

"I'm telling you, put an end to this thing with Márinka – no talking back, that's what I want and that is that, her mother is neither good nor trustworthy," said Mrs. Bavor in a much more agitated voice while recording the numbers drawn by Václav. "So there – and now your left hand! And that landlords' girl keeps coming over here! She says she wants you to forgive her that they didn't invite you yesterday; supposedly she was ashamed – her and ashamed! – and the old woman, she says, forgot and then they felt very bad about it. But I know what they're up to; they are up to their eyes in debt and today they heard from that garrulous customer – oh, yes, you don't know yet that I hit the jackpot –"

"The jackpot –," stammered Václav again.

"Yes – I hit the mark – we'll be getting a few thousand ..."

"Is that true, Mother?" exclaimed Václav clasping his hands.

"Has your mother ever lied to you?"

Václav sprang over the counter and started to hug and kiss her.

"Well – well, you crazy fellow, you'll never grow up," responded Mrs. Bavor. "I knew it had to come one day! But you – you discipline yourself and finish your studies!"

Václav's eyes sparkled. He jumped up and grabbed a bunch of keys from the wall.

"Where are you going?"

"To the attic."

"To do what?"

"To make plans for my life!"

14 From a Happy Home

The landlord paced back and forth across the room. He was still in his early morning attire dressed only in long johns without suspenders. His chest was bare, his still uncombed

hair stuck out in all directions. His square and wrinkled face showed bewilderment, his dangling arms were swinging aimlessly around his body while he walked.

The landlady, also in her undergarments, stood beside the chest of drawers pretending to be dusting, yet her every movement testified to the same bewilderment.

The cause of the bewilderment was a third person, sitting here on a chair by the table. An insider would grasp the situation in an instant. The unknown man belonged, judging by the shape of his face, undoubtedly to the nation from which we know so far only one person who returned the money he had gained, the biblical figure, Judas. The unknown man was evidently no stranger to the Eber household, judging by how he kept putting his shabby hat on his bald head which was edged by thin gray strands, and taking it off again as if it was his own home; he was drumming on the table and unscrupulously spitting on the floor. His eyes suggested conscious superiority and a scant impertinent smile played around the corners of his mouth and his drooping lips made no effort to conceal it.

Suddenly he gave a twitch, leaned on the table and got up.

"Well, I can see that here, too, I've thrown my money away," he said in a resounding voice. "But I can take care of myself, you won't get another kreutzer out of me!"

The landlady turned to him and with a forced, gracious smile said, "Only fifty guilders more, Mr. Menke, you'll help us out and we'll be grateful to you, you'll see!"

"What might you mean by 'grateful'?" the Jew made a wry face. "I'd be grateful myself if someone gave me fifty guilders."

"But we are worth it for you, Mr. Menke, aren't we, there's our house and –"

"House! There are many houses in Prague and many landlords, too, I know that; but do you know who the landlord of your house really is? I have your rent schedule, hmm, but what good is it to me if I get no percentage from it? If I don't get my interest by Tuesday, I'm going to the president!" and he walked to the door.

"But Mr. Menke –"

"No – I've got children and can't be deprived of my money. Good day to you!" He walked away leaving the door open behind him.

The landlord swung his arms and moved his lips as if to

say something; the landlady leaped angrily to the door and slammed it shut.

The door to the other room, up till now ajar, opened and in came Miss Matylda. She was clad in an underskirt and was yawning a bit while looking listlessly around the room.

"I don't know why you'd even talk to someone like him," she remarked blandly. "I would throw him out."

Mr. Eber was standing in front of the mirror combing his hair. His daughter's words upset him and he turned swiftly upon her. "Be quiet! What do you know about that!" he snapped back sharply.

"Fine, all right" stated Miss Matylda, not letting herself get thrown off balance. She stepped to the window yawning most contentedly into the beautiful morning.

The landlady was noticeably quiet. She was now dusting the chest of drawers with such vigour that it sighed.

There was a long silence while Mr. Eber was getting himself dressed and his spouse was flitting about the room picking things up here and there and then immediately putting them down again. Mr. Eber knew that the situation could not go on like this for too long, so he finally began to break the silence himself.

"Why don't you pour me some coffee, woman – you know that it's almost time for me to go to the office!" he said in his calmest voice.

"It's not warmed up yet," replied the landlady dryly, opening the door of the tall wardrobe.

"Warmed up – well, you're not giving me warmed up coffee from yesterday, are you? For goodness sake!"

"And why not! Do you bring home enough so that we can be cooking in the kitchen all day? Earn yourself a fresh one!"

Miss Matylda turned away from the window and sat down folding her hands in her lap. She took turns looking at her father and then her mother and it was evident she was beginning to be amused. Knowing his spouse well, Mr. Eber tried a different tack, not wishing to start a fight on top of everything. "I wonder what we're having for dinner today," he said, as if breakfast had never been mentioned.

"Dumplings with horseradish sauce," came the biting response.

Mr. Eber could not stand dumplings with horseradish sauce. He observed her deliberate spitefulness and started to feel vexed.

"And why today of all days should we have that damned meal, if I may ask, Madam?" he uttered with great effort.

"Because! We're washing today and when we're washing, I don't cook anything else!" The landlady was looking for something in the wardrobe and, unable to find it right away, she began forcefully pulling things down from their hooks and throwing them onto the floor.

"Ah – washing all day! And where am I supposed to go in the meantime?"

"Wherever you please? What a wonderful parent you are anyway, not taking our child out for a walk the whole year round, why don't you then go some place with Valinka for half a day?"

"And that's it?" Mr. Eber asked in a hoarse, by now extremely infuriated voice.

"Well, maybe you can stand on a corner somewhere and beg!" she stepped into the wardrobe itself while saying this as she was unable to reach what she was after. "With your wits we'll soon have no other choice; you just wait till I poison myself, even if I should poison myself with glass! Now we have to make things right with Matylda, if she even succeeds in finding someone who'd fall in love with her – why did you have to bicker the Bavor fellow out of the office? Playing a bigwig and being a nobody –" she didn't finish her sentence; Mr. Eber, not able to control himself any longer, leapt forward pushing his spouse deep inside the wardrobe, slammed the door and turned the key.

Miss Matylda clasped her hands in joy.

A tremendous pounding and banging came out of the wardrobe, which also began to rock. Mr. Eber grabbed a glass and flung it against the wardrobe where it smashed. Miss Matylda again happily clasped her hands in glee.

The din inside grew louder still. Mr. Eber hastily put on his coat, took his hat in his hand, and then hesitated. Perhaps he was not sure whether he should just unlock the wardrobe now.

Miss Matylda noticed his hesitation and said quickly, "Just leave her there! She should've been quiet!"

"You're right," agreed her father. "Let her out when I'm somewhere on the street. I'm going!"

And out he went. At the same moment, though, a thought flashed through Miss Matylda. She leaped to the wardrobe

and, as her mother, pale as death with anger, briskly stepped out, said, "He's running away – hurry!" But the landlady didn't need to be told a second time, and she dashed to
the door quick as an arrow, followed by her daughter, who
was not about to miss anything.

The landlady grabbed a broom in the kitchen and bolted
out to the courtyard gallery. Mr. Eber was just proceeding
down the stairs and passed a maid who was busy washing
the stairs. "Kick the bucket over him, pour it on top of him!"
the landlady shouted.

Her husband sped up his steps to a perilous haste. He had
already made it into the courtyard when the broom whirred
past his ears, luckily missing him. Having seen that, the
landlady tore her bonnet off her head and flung it onto her
running husband. She started to scream so that it rang
throughout the entire house. "Murderer, thief! Just look at
you and I'd like to see you without all that flannel around
you, – you wretch! What a husband I got for myself, three
hundred guilders a year and he thinks he's something. Pooh
on a husband like that! Don't you come back for another
week, I'm telling you!"

Mr. Eber, though, having already disappeared through
the passageway, did not hear this good advice. The whole
scene was over so fast that the tenants rushing to their windows could see nothing but Miss Matylda, who had been
watching from the door, putting her arms around her mother in a joyous embrace!

15 The End of the Day

Although Josefinka's wedding took place early on Sunday
morning, the courtyard was full of curious neighbours, and
a large crowd had assembled even outside the house. They
were observing everything very closely and concluded that
this was a rather "pale wedding".

By this they did not mean it was plain, since Josefinka's
groom had not spared anything, the bride had a fine silk
dress and there were a number of carriages on top of that,
yet the neighbours were right. All the faces, well known to

them, were indeed notably pale today as if God knows what had happened before they set out. That the bride was pale came as no surprise – "pale bride, cheerful wife" – but she was followed by her agitated pale groom with the ever-colourless Miss Klára as her bridesmaid, and as chance would have it, the other faces were also marked by the same pallor. Even the normally beaming round face of the doctor, who was the witness, was today somewhat peculiar. Only Václav, the best man, was laughing and joking as usual; but everybody knew he held nothing sacred.

In the afternoon the doctor stood in front of the house and pulled on his gloves, now and then turning to the passageway as if expecting someone. Then all at once Václav, completely dressed up, came out of the shop and approached him.

"Out for a walk, Doctor?"

"Yes – to Stromovka Park!"

"All by yourself?"

"Yes – actually, Mrs. Lakmus is also going that way!"

"Oh, I see, and Miss Klára! She looked good today." The doctor took a quick look down the street. "And whereabouts are you off to?"

"To Šárka Valley."

"In someone's company, of course – perhaps with Márinka?"

"Well, actually not," Václav smiled, "With the landlords."

Women's voices could be heard through the passageway; at its end the Lakmuses met the Ebers.

"With the landlords?" marvelled the doctor. "I hope you don't really want to become entangled in an affair – my oh my!"

"Oh, Doctor, I do know what I'm doing – I'm only avenging our sex. You are avenging it too, aren't you, Doctor?"

The doctor's eyes blinked in bewilderment. He opened his mouth as if to answer and closed it without a word. He cleared his throat slightly and said, "Shh, they're coming!"...